D1135246

everyday
mexican

This is a Parragon book
First published in 2007

Parragon
Queen Street House
4 Queen Street
Bath BA1 1HE, UK

Copyright © Parragon Books Ltd 2007
Designed by Terry Jeavons & Company

ISBN 978-1-4054-9396-3

All rights reserved. No part of this publication may be reproduced, stored in a retrieval system or transmitted, in any form or by any means, electronic, mechanical, photocopying, recording or otherwise, without the prior permission of the copyright holder.

Printed in China

This book uses metric and imperial measurements. Follow the same units of measurement throughout; do not mix metric and imperial. All spoon measurements are level, unless otherwise stated: teaspoons are assumed to be 5ml, and tablespoons are assumed to be 15ml. Unless otherwise stated, milk is assumed to be whole, eggs and individual fruits such as bananas are medium, and pepper is freshly ground black pepper.

Recipes using raw or very lightly cooked eggs should be avoided by infants, the elderly, pregnant women, convalescents and anyone suffering from an illness. Pregnant and breast-feeding women are advised to avoid eating peanuts and peanut products.

everyday
mexican

introduction

The cuisine of Mexico is diverse and extraordinary and is fusion food at its most literal, having evolved from a complex layering of cultures. It began with the Indian civilizations and in later centuries was built on by the Spanish conquest as well as other European rulers and influences.

The soul of Mexican food lies in its ancient roots – Aztec, Toltec, Zapotec, Ohnec and Mayan. From these roots come the deeply coloured, rich sauces made of mild and hot chillies, seeds, herbs and vegetables that are so characteristic of Mexican cuisine. Long-stewed meats are also a feature, while the broth that results

forms the basis for the soups that fuel everyday life and is used to add flavour and depth to stews, and to bean and rice dishes. Fish are flavoured with spicy pastes or chillies and served wrapped in tortillas or fragrant leaves.

To this ancient cuisine making use of the country's indigenous foods, the Spanish settlers added their own touch, not least of which was the pig – a useful source of meat now very popular in Mexican cooking, while the fat that comes from pork enabled frying to be used as an alternative cooking method. In addition, the Spanish brought wheat, used to make tortillas and crusty bread rolls, and domestic animals – cows, sheep and goats – whose milk was used to make cheese.

The name Mexico conjures up a picture of sunshine, heat, colour and fiesta, and Mexican food reflects this – indeed, meals are a never-ending fiesta. The main meal is served Spanish style in the afternoon and follows a light breakfast of hot chocolate or coffee

with sweet rolls or cinnamon-sprinkled churros, or a substantial 'brunch', often consisting of one of the country's well-known egg dishes. For in between there are markets and cafés selling tantalizing snacks. Eat Mexican-style, and soak up that party atmosphere!

something light

This chapter has a selection of some of Mexico's best soup and appetizer recipes, which you can use to form part of a Mexican-style feast for the family or serve on their own when you want a light lunch or supper dish that has just a little more character than the usual sandwich.

The soups are certainly packed with enough goodness to keep you full of energy, ranging from a light but very nutritious chilled avocado soup to Pozole, a protein-packed meal-in-a-bowl made from pork, chicken and hominy (maize kernels) simmered in a rich stock. Mexican soups are served with plenty of garnishes, from a spoonful of soured cream, chunks of lime and freshly chopped herbs to more complicated salsas, which complement the soup perfectly so are worth the extra effort.

Cheese and beans are a big feature of Mexican cuisine, and form the basis of Mexico's many exciting variations on the sandwich – tortillas, tostadas, quesadillas, tortas and molletes. Fish and seafood are also very much in evidence, served in surprising ways – plump, juicy prawns with smooth, sweet mango and a hint of mild chilli, for example, an unusual but delightful combination. And you'll find some new and interesting ways to serve eggs, too.

mexican vegetable soup with tortilla chips

ingredients

SERVES 4–6

2 tbsp vegetable or virgin olive oil

1 onion, finely chopped

4 garlic cloves, finely chopped

$1/4$–$1/2$ tsp ground cumin

2–3 tsp mild chilli powder, such as ancho or New Mexico

1 carrot, sliced

1 waxy potato, diced

350 g/12 oz diced fresh or canned tomatoes

1 courgette, diced

$1/4$ small cabbage, shredded

1 litre/32 fl oz vegetable or chicken stock or water

1 corn cob, the kernels cut off the cob

about 10 green or string beans, cut into bite-size lengths

salt and pepper

to serve

4–6 tbsp chopped fresh coriander

salsa of your choice or chopped fresh chilli, to taste

tortilla chips

method

Heat the oil in a heavy-based frying pan or saucepan. Add the onion and garlic and cook for a few minutes until softened, then sprinkle in the cumin and chilli powder. Stir in the carrot, potato, tomatoes, courgette and cabbage and cook for 2 minutes, stirring the mixture occasionally.

Pour in the stock. Cover and cook over medium heat for 20 minutes, or until the vegetables are tender.

Add extra water if necessary, then stir in the corn and beans and cook for a further 5–10 minutes, or until the beans are tender. Season the soup to taste with salt and pepper, bearing in mind that the tortilla chips may be salty.

Ladle the soup into soup bowls and sprinkle each portion with chopped coriander. Top with a little salsa, then add a handful of tortilla chips.

chilled avocado
& coriander soup

ingredients

SERVES 4

4 ripe avocados

1 shallot or 2 spring onions, finely chopped

850 ml/28 fl oz cold chicken or strongly flavoured vegetable stock

150 ml/5 fl oz soured cream, plus extra to serve

2 tbsp tomato purée

few drops of Tabasco sauce, or to taste

juice of 1 lime, or to taste

1 tbsp tequila (optional)

1 tbsp chopped fresh coriander, plus extra to garnish

salt and pepper

method

Cut the avocados in half lengthways and twist the two halves in opposite directions to separate. Stab the stone with the point of a sharp knife and lift out of the avocado.

Peel, then coarsely chop the avocado halves and place in a food processor or blender with the shallot, stock, soured cream, tomato purée, Tabasco, lime juice, tequila, chopped coriander and salt and pepper. Process until smooth, then taste and add more Tabasco, lime juice and salt and pepper if necessary.

Transfer the mixture to a large bowl, cover and chill in the refrigerator for at least 2 hours, or until thoroughly chilled.

Divide the soup between 4 chilled serving bowls and serve, topped with a spoonful of soured cream and garnished with extra chopped coriander.

easy gazpacho

ingredients

SERVES 4

1 small cucumber, peeled
    and chopped
2 red peppers, deseeded and
    chopped
2 green peppers, deseeded
    and chopped
2 garlic cloves, chopped
1 fresh basil sprig
600 ml/20 fl oz strained
    tomatoes
1 tbsp extra-virgin olive oil
1 tbsp red wine vinegar
1 tbsp balsamic vinegar
300 ml/10 fl oz vegetable
    stock
2 tbsp lemon juice
salt and pepper

to serve

2 tbsp diced, peeled cucumber
2 tbsp finely chopped red onion
2 tbsp each finely chopped
    red and green pepper
ice cubes
4 fresh basil sprigs
fresh crusty bread

method

Put the cucumber, peppers, garlic and basil in a food
processor and process for $1^{1}/_{2}$ minutes. Add the
strained tomatoes, olive oil and both kinds of vinegar
and process until smooth.

Pour in the vegetable stock and lemon juice and stir.
Transfer the mixture to a large bowl. Season to taste with
salt and pepper. Cover with clingfilm and chill in the
refrigerator for at least 2 hours.

To serve, prepare the cucumber, onion and peppers, then
place in small serving dishes or arrange decoratively on a
plate. Place ice cubes in 4 large soup bowls. Stir the soup
and ladle it into the bowls. Garnish with the basil sprigs
and serve with the prepared vegetables and chunks of
fresh crusty bread.

beef & bean soup

ingredients

SERVES 4

2 tbsp vegetable oil

1 large onion, finely chopped

2 garlic cloves, finely chopped

1 green pepper, deseeded
    and sliced

2 carrots, sliced

400 g/14 oz canned
    black-eyed beans

225 g/8 oz fresh minced beef

1 tsp each of ground cumin,
    chilli powder and paprika

1/4 cabbage, sliced

225 g/8 oz tomatoes, peeled
    and chopped

600 ml/20 fl oz beef stock

salt and pepper

method

Heat the oil in a large saucepan over medium heat. Add the onion and garlic and cook, stirring frequently, for 5 minutes, or until softened. Add the pepper and carrots and cook for a further 5 minutes.

Meanwhile, drain the beans, reserving the liquid from the can. Place two-thirds of the beans, reserving the remainder, in a food processor or blender with the bean liquid and process until smooth.

Add the minced beef to the pan and cook, stirring constantly to break up any lumps, until well browned. Add the spices and cook, stirring, for 2 minutes. Add the cabbage, tomatoes, stock and puréed beans and season to taste with salt and pepper. Bring to the boil, then reduce the heat, cover and simmer for 15 minutes, or until the vegetables are tender.

Stir in the reserved beans, cover and simmer for a further 5 minutes. Ladle the soup into warmed soup bowls and serve.

pozole

ingredients

SERVES 4

450 g/1 lb pork for stewing,
  such as lean belly
1/2 small chicken
about 2 litres/64 fl oz water
1 chicken stock cube
1 whole garlic bulb, divided
  into cloves but not peeled
1 onion, chopped
2 bay leaves
450 g/1 lb canned or cooked
  hominy or chickpeas
1/4–1/2 tsp ground cumin
salt and pepper

to serve

1/2 small cabbage, thinly
  shredded
fried pork skin
dried oregano leaves
dried chilli flakes
lime wedges
tortilla chips (optional)

method

Place the pork and chicken in a large saucepan. Add enough water to fill the pan. (Do not worry about having too much stock – it can be used in other dishes, and freezes well.)

Bring to the boil, then skim off the scum that rises to the surface. Reduce the heat and add the stock cube, garlic, onion and bay leaves. Simmer, covered, over medium–low heat for 1 1/2–2 hours, or until the pork and chicken are both tender and cooked through.

Using a slotted spoon, remove the pork and chicken from the soup and set aside to cool. When cool enough to handle, remove the chicken flesh from the bones and cut into small pieces. Cut the pork into bite-size pieces. Set aside.

Skim the fat off the soup and discard the bay leaves. Add the hominy or chickpeas, cumin and salt and pepper to taste. Bring to the boil.

To serve, place a little pork and chicken in soup bowls. Top with cabbage, fried pork skin, oregano and chilli flakes, then spoon in the hot soup. Serve with lime wedges and tortilla chips, if wished.

chicken, avocado & chipotle soup

ingredients

SERVES 4

1.5 litres/48 fl oz chicken stock

2–3 garlic cloves, finely chopped

1–2 dried chipotle chillies, cut into very thin strips

1 avocado

lime or lemon juice, for tossing

3–5 spring onions, thinly sliced

350–400 g/12–14 oz cooked chicken breast meat, torn or cut into shreds or thin strips

2 tbsp chopped fresh coriander

to serve

1 lime, cut into wedges

handful of tortilla chips (optional)

method

Place the stock in a large, heavy-based saucepan with the garlic and chillies and bring to the boil.

Meanwhile, cut the avocado in half around the stone. Twist apart, then remove the stone with a knife. Carefully peel off the skin, dice the flesh and toss in lime juice to prevent discoloration.

Arrange the spring onions, chicken, avocado and coriander in the bottom of 4 soup bowls or in a large serving bowl.

Ladle hot stock over and serve with lime wedges and a handful of tortilla chips, if wished.

mexican fish & roasted tomato soup

ingredients

SERVES 4

5 ripe tomatoes

5 garlic cloves, unpeeled

500 g/1 lb 2 oz red snapper,
cut into chunks

1 litre/32 fl oz fish stock or
water mixed with 1–2 fish
stock cubes

2–3 tbsp olive oil

1 onion, chopped

2 fresh green chillies, such as
serrano, deseeded and
thinly sliced

lime wedges, to serve

method

Heat an unoiled heavy-based frying pan. Add the
tomatoes and garlic and char over high heat or under a
preheated hot grill. The skins of the vegetables should
blacken and the flesh inside should be tender.
Alternatively, place the tomatoes and garlic in a roasting
pan and bake in a preheated oven, 190°C/375°F/Gas
Mark 5, for 40 minutes.

Let the tomatoes and garlic cool, then remove the skins
and coarsely chop, combining them with any juices from
the frying pan or roasting pan. Set aside.

Poach the fish in the stock in a deep frying pan or
saucepan over medium heat until it is just opaque and
slightly firm. Remove from the heat and set aside.

Heat the oil in a separate deep frying pan or saucepan.
Add the onion and cook for 5 minutes, or until softened.
Strain in the cooking liquid from the fish, then stir in the
tomatoes and garlic.

Bring to the boil, then reduce the heat and simmer for
5 minutes to combine the flavours. Add the chillies.

Divide chunks of the poached fish between soup bowls,
ladle over the hot soup and serve with lime wedges for
squeezing over the top.

spicy fragrant black bean chilli

ingredients

SERVES 4

400 g/14 oz dried black
    beans
2 tbsp olive oil
1 onion, chopped
5 garlic cloves, coarsely
    chopped
2 bacon slices, diced (optional)
1/2–1 tsp ground cumin
1/2–1 tsp mild red chilli powder
1 red pepper, diced
1 carrot, diced
400 g/14 oz fresh tomatoes,
    diced, or canned, chopped
1 bunch fresh coriander,
    coarsely chopped
salt and pepper

method

Soak the beans overnight, then drain. Place in a saucepan, cover with water and bring to the boil. Boil for 10 minutes, then reduce the heat and simmer for 1 1/2 hours, or until tender. Drain well, reserving 250 ml/8 fl oz of the cooking liquid.

Heat the oil in a frying pan. Add the onion and garlic and cook for 2 minutes, stirring. Add the bacon, if using, and cook, stirring occasionally, until the bacon is cooked and the onion is softened.

Stir in the cumin and chilli powder and continue to cook for a moment or two. Add the red pepper, carrot and tomatoes. Cook over medium heat for 5 minutes.

Add half the coriander and the beans and their reserved liquid. Season to taste with salt and pepper. Simmer for 30–45 minutes, or until very flavourful and thickened.

Stir in the remaining coriander, adjust the seasoning and serve at once.

prawn &
mango cocktail

ingredients

SERVES 4

6 cherry tomatoes

1 large ripe mango

1 fresh mild green chilli,
    deseeded and finely
    chopped

juice of 1 lime

1 tbsp chopped fresh
    coriander

salt and pepper

400 g/14 oz shelled jumbo
    prawns, cooked

fresh coriander, chopped,
    to garnish

method

Place the tomatoes in a heatproof bowl and pour over enough boiling water to cover. Let stand for 1–2 minutes, then remove the tomatoes with a slotted spoon, peel off the skins and refresh in cold water. Dice the flesh and place in a large, non-metallic bowl.

Slice the mango lengthways on either side of the flat central seed. Peel the two mango pieces and cut the flesh into chunks. Slice and peel any remaining flesh around the stone, then cut into chunks. Add to the tomatoes with any juice.

Add the chilli, lime juice, chopped coriander and salt and pepper to taste. Cover and chill in the refrigerator for 2 hours to allow the flavours to develop.

Remove the dish from the refrigerator. Fold the prawns gently into the mango mixture and divide between 4 serving dishes. Garnish with chopped coriander and serve at once.

seafood cocktail
à la Veracruz

ingredients

SERVES 6

1 litre/32 fl oz fish stock or
    water mixed with 1 fish
    stock cube

2 bay leaves

1 onion, chopped

3–5 garlic cloves, cut into
    big chunks

675 g/1 lb 8 oz mixed raw
    seafood, such as prawns
    in their shells, scallops,
    squid rings, pieces of
    squid tentacles, etc

175 ml/6 fl oz tomato ketchup

4 tbsp Mexican hot sauce

generous pinch of ground
    cumin

6–8 tbsp chopped fresh
    coriander

4 tbsp lime juice, plus extra
    for tossing

salt

1 avocado, to garnish

method

Place the stock in a large, heavy-based saucepan and add the bay leaves, half the onion and all the garlic. Bring to the boil, then reduce the heat and simmer for 10 minutes, or until the onion and garlic are soft and the stock tastes flavourful.

Add the seafood in the order of the amount of cooking time required. Most small pieces of shellfish take a very short time to cook and can be added together. Cook for 1 minute, then remove the pan from the heat. Allow the seafood to finish cooking by standing in the cooling stock.

When the stock has cooled, remove the seafood from the stock with a slotted spoon. Shell the prawns and any other shellfish. Set the stock aside until required.

Combine the ketchup, hot sauce and cumin in a bowl. Reserve a quarter of the sauce mixture for serving. Add the seafood to the bowl with the remaining onion, coriander, lime juice and about 250 ml/8 fl oz of the reserved fish stock. Stir carefully to mix and season to taste with salt.

Peel and pit the avocado, then dice the flesh. Toss gently in lime juice to prevent discoloration. Serve the cocktail in individual bowls, garnished with the avocado and topped with a spoonful of the reserved sauce.

cheese & bean quesadillas

ingredients

SERVES 4–6

8 flour tortillas (see page 206)

vegetable oil, for oiling

1/2 quantity refried beans
(see page 202), warmed
with a little water

200 g/7 oz Cheddar cheese,
grated

1 onion, chopped

1/2 bunch fresh coriander
leaves, chopped, plus
extra leaves to garnish
(optional)

1 quantity salsa cruda (see
page 168)

method

First make the tortillas pliable, by warming them gently in a lightly oiled non-stick frying pan.

Remove the tortillas from the pan and quickly spread with a layer of warmed beans. Top each tortilla with grated cheese, onion, coriander and a spoonful of salsa. Roll up tightly.

Just before serving, heat the non-stick frying pan over medium heat, sprinkling lightly with a drop or two of water. Add the tortilla rolls, cover the pan and heat through until the cheese melts. Allow to lightly brown, if wished.

Remove from the pan and slice each roll, on the diagonal, into about 4 bite-size pieces. Serve the dish at once, garnished with coriander, if wished.

nachos

ingredients

SERVES 6

175 g/6 oz tortilla chips

1 quantity warmed refried
   beans (see page 202)
   or 400 g/14 oz canned
   refried beans, warmed

2 tbsp finely chopped bottled
   jalapeño chillies

200 g/7 oz canned or bottled
   pimientos or roasted
   peppers, drained and
   finely sliced

salt and pepper

115 g/4 oz Gruyère cheese,
   grated

115 g/4 oz Cheddar cheese,
   grated

method

Spread the tortilla chips out over the bottom of a large,
shallow, ovenproof dish or roasting pan. Cover with the
warmed refried beans. Sprinkle over the chillies and
pimientos and season to taste with salt and pepper.
Mix the cheeses together in a bowl and sprinkle on top.

Bake in a preheated oven, 200°C/400°F/Gas Mark 6,
for 5–8 minutes, or until the cheese is bubbling and
melted. Serve at once.

roasted cheese
with salsa

ingredients

SERVES 4

225 g/8 oz mozzarella, fresh
    romano or Mexican queso
    oaxaca cheese
175 ml/6 fl oz salsa cruda
    (see page 168)
    or other good salsa
1/2–1 onion, finely chopped
8 soft corn tortillas, to serve

method

To warm the tortillas ready for serving, heat an unoiled
non-stick frying pan, add a tortilla and heat through,
sprinkling with a few drops of water as it heats. Wrap in
foil or a clean tea towel to keep warm. Repeat with the
other tortillas.

Cut the cheese into chunks or slabs and arrange them
in a shallow ovenproof dish or in individual dishes.

Spoon the salsa over the cheese to cover and place in a
preheated oven, 200°C/400°F/Gas Mark 6, or under a
grill preheated to medium. Cook until the cheese melts
and is bubbling, lightly browning in places.

Sprinkle with chopped onion to taste and serve with the
warmed tortillas for dipping. Serve immediately as the
melted cheese turns stringy when cold and becomes
difficult to eat.

tamales

ingredients

SERVES 4–6

8–10 corn husks or several
    banana leaves, cut into
    30-cm/12-inch squares
6 tbsp shortening
1/2 tsp salt
pinch of sugar
pinch of ground cumin
225 g/8 oz masa harina
1/2 tsp baking powder
about 225 ml/8 fl oz beef,
    chicken or vegetable stock

filling

115 g/4 oz cooked sweetcorn
    kernels, mixed with grated
    cheese and chopped fresh
    green chilli, or pork simmered
    in a mild chilli sauce

to serve

shredded lettuce
tomato wedges
salsa of your choice

method

If using corn husks, soak in enough hot water to cover
for at least 3 hours or overnight. If using banana leaves,
warm them by placing over an open flame for just a few
seconds, to make them pliable.

To make the tamale dough, beat the shortening until fluffy in
a bowl, then beat in the salt, sugar, cumin, masa harina and
baking powder until the mixture resembles very fine crumbs.

Add the stock very gradually, in several batches,
beating until the mixture becomes fluffy and resembles
whipped cream.

Spread 1–2 tablespoons of the tamale mixture on either
a soaked and drained corn husk or a piece of pliable
heated banana leaf.

Spoon in the filling. Fold the sides of the husks or leaves
over the filling to enclose. Wrap each pocket in a square
of foil and arrange in a steamer.

Pour enough hot water into the bottom of the steamer,
cover and boil. Steam for 40–60 minutes, topping up
the water in the bottom of the steamer when needed.
Remove the tamales and serve with shredded lettuce,
tomato wedges and salsa.

molletes

ingredients

SERVES 4

4 bread rolls
1 tbsp vegetable oil, plus
    extra for brushing
400 g/14 oz refried beans
    (see page 202) or canned
1 onion, chopped
3 garlic cloves, chopped
3 bacon slices, cut into small
    pieces, or about 85 g/3 oz
    chorizo sausage, diced
225 g/8 oz diced fresh or
    canned tomatoes
1/4–1/2 tsp ground cumin
250 g/9 oz grated cheese

cabbage salad

1/2 cabbage, thinly sliced
2 tbsp sliced pickled jalapeño
    chillies
1 tbsp extra-virgin olive oil
3 tbsp cider vinegar
1/4 tsp dried oregano
salt and pepper

method

To make the salad, combine the cabbage with the chillies, olive oil and vinegar in a bowl. Add the oregano and salt and pepper to taste. Set aside.

Cut the rolls in half and remove a little of the crumb to make space for the filling. Brush the rolls all over with vegetable oil. Arrange on a baking sheet and bake in a preheated oven, 200°C/ 400°F/Gas Mark 6, for 10–15 minutes, or until the rolls are crisp and light golden.

Meanwhile, place the beans in a saucepan and heat through gently with enough water to thin them to a smooth paste.

Heat the 1 tablespoon of vegetable oil in a frying pan. Add the onion, garlic and bacon or chorizo and cook until the bacon or chorizo is browned and the onion is softened. Add the tomatoes and simmer, stirring, until they break down to form a thick sauce. Add the warmed beans and stir to combine with the mixture. Stir in the cumin to taste. Set aside.

Remove the rolls from the oven; keep the oven on. Fill the rolls with the warm bean mixture, then top with the cheese and close up tightly. Return to the baking sheet and heat through in the oven until the cheese melts. Open the rolls up, spoon in a little of the salad and serve.

tortas

ingredients

SERVES 4

4 crusty rolls, such as French
    rolls or bocadillos

melted butter or olive oil, for
    brushing

225 g/8 oz refried beans or
    canned

350 g/12 oz shredded cooked
    chicken, browned chorizo
    sausage pieces, sliced
    ham and cheese or any
    leftover cooked meat you
    have to hand

1 ripe tomato, sliced or diced

1 small onion, finely chopped

2 tbsp chopped fresh
    coriander

1 avocado, pitted, peeled,
    sliced and tossed with
    lime juice

4–6 tbsp soured cream or
    Greek-style yogurt

salsa of your choice

handful of shredded lettuce

method

Cut the rolls in half and, using your fingers, remove a
little of the crumb to make space for the filling.

Brush the outside and inside of the rolls with butter and
toast, on both sides, in a hot griddle pan or frying pan
for a few minutes until crisp. Alternatively, bake in a
preheated oven, 200°C/400°F/Gas Mark 6, until
lightly toasted.

Meanwhile, place the beans in a saucepan with a tiny
amount of water and heat through gently.

When the rolls are heated, spread one half of each roll
generously with the beans, then top with a layer of cooked
meat. Top with tomato, onion, coriander and avocado.

Generously spread soured cream onto the other side of
each roll. Drizzle the salsa over the filling, add a little
shredded lettuce, then sandwich the two sides of each
roll together and press tightly. Serve immediately.

chicken tortilla flutes with guacamole

ingredients

SERVES 4

8 soft corn tortillas
350 g/12 oz cooked chicken, diced
1 tsp mild chilli powder
1 onion, chopped
2 tbsp finely chopped fresh coriander
salt
1–2 tbsp soured cream
vegetable oil, for frying

to serve

guacamole (see page 152)
salsa of your choice

method

Heat the tortillas in an unoiled non-stick frying pan in a stack, moving the tortillas from the top to the bottom so that they warm evenly. Wrap in foil or a clean tea towel to keep them warm.

Place the chicken in a large bowl with the chilli powder, half the chopped onion and coriander and salt to taste. Add enough soured cream to bind the mixture together.

Arrange 2 corn tortillas on the work surface so that they are overlapping, then spoon some of the filling down the centre. Roll up very tightly and secure in place with a cocktail stick or two. Repeat with the remaining tortillas and filling.

Heat enough oil for frying in a deep frying pan until hot and fry the rolls until golden and crisp. Carefully remove the rolls from the oil and drain on kitchen paper.

Serve with the guacamole, salsa and the remaining onion and coriander.

stuffed tortillas

ingredients

SERVES 2

4 sausages

4 large wheat or corn tortillas, or 8 small ones

salad, to garnish

salsa

2 red peppers, deseeded and cut into quarters

325 g/11¹/₂ oz canned red kidney beans, drained, rinsed and drained again

4 large tomatoes, chopped

1 large onion, chopped

1 garlic clove, chopped

1 tbsp lime juice

1 tbsp chopped fresh basil

salt and pepper

to serve

shredded lettuce

slices of fresh tomato

soured cream

method

To make the salsa, cook the red peppers, skin-side up, under a preheated grill for about 5 minutes, or until the skins are blackened and charred. Transfer them to a plastic bag, seal the bag and set to one side.

Put the kidney beans, tomatoes, onion, garlic, lime juice and basil into a large bowl. Season with salt and pepper and mix until well combined. Take the red pepper quarters from the plastic bag and remove the blackened skins. Chop the flesh into small pieces and add it to the kidney bean mixture.

Grill the sausages for 10–12 minutes, or until cooked right through, turning occasionally. Meanwhile, warm the tortillas in an unoiled non-stick frying pan in a stack, moving the tortillas from the top to the bottom so that they warm evenly. Wrap in foil or a clean tea towel to keep them warm.

Cut the sausages into slices. Fill the tortillas with sausage slices, kidney bean salsa, shredded lettuce, tomato slices and soured cream. Serve at once with a salad garnish.

vegetable tostadas

ingredients

SERVES 4

4 soft corn tortillas

2–3 tbsp or vegetable oil, plus
extra for frying

2 potatoes, diced

1 carrot, diced

3 garlic cloves, finely chopped

1 red pepper, deseeded and
diced

1 tsp mild chilli powder

1 tsp paprika

$1/2$ tsp ground cumin

3–4 ripe tomatoes, diced

115 g/4 oz green beans,
blanched and cut into
bite-size lengths

dried oregano

400 g/14 oz cooked black
beans, drained

225 g/8 oz crumbled feta
cheese

3–4 romaine lettuce leaves,
shredded

3–4 spring onions, thinly
sliced

method

To make the tostadas, fry the tortillas in a small amount of oil in a non-stick frying pan until crisp. Set aside.

Heat the remaining oil in the pan. Add the potatoes and carrot and cook for 10 minutes, or until softened. Add the garlic, red pepper, chilli powder, paprika and cumin. Cook for 2–3 minutes, or until the peppers have softened.

Add the tomatoes, green beans and several large pinches of dried oregano. Cook for 8–10 minutes, or until the vegetables are tender and form a sauce-like mixture. The mixture should not be too dry; add a little water if necessary to keep it moist.

Heat the black beans in a saucepan with a tiny amount of water and keep warm. Reheat the tostadas under a preheated hot grill.

Layer the beans over the hot tostadas, then sprinkle with the cheese and top with a few spoonfuls of the hot vegetables in sauce. Sprinkle each tostada with the lettuce and spring onions and serve at once.

spinach & mushroom chimichangas

ingredients

SERVES 4

2 tbsp olive oil

1 large onion, finely chopped

225 g/8 oz small mushrooms,
  finely sliced

2 fresh mild green chillies,
  deseeded and finely
  chopped

2 garlic cloves, finely chopped

250 g/9 oz spinach leaves,
  torn into pieces if large

175 g/6 oz Cheddar cheese,
  grated

8 flour tortillas (see page
  206), warmed

vegetable oil, for deep-frying

method

Heat the oil in a large, heavy-based frying pan. Add the onion and cook over medium heat for 5 minutes, or until softened.

Add the mushrooms, chillies and garlic and cook for 5 minutes, or until the mushrooms are lightly browned. Add the spinach and cook, stirring, for 1–2 minutes, or until just wilted. Add the cheese and stir until just melted.

Spoon an equal quantity of the mixture into the centre of each tortilla. Fold in two opposite sides of each tortilla to cover the filling, then roll up to enclose it completely.

Heat the oil for deep-frying in a deep-fryer or large, deep saucepan to 180–190°C/350–375°F, or until a cube of bread browns in 30 seconds. Deep-fry the chimichangas two at a time, turning once, for 5–6 minutes, or until crisp and golden. Drain on kitchen paper before serving.

cheese enchiladas with mole flavours

ingredients

SERVES 4

8 soft corn tortillas

vegetable oil, for oiling

500 ml/16 fl oz mole poblano
(see page 158)
or bottled mole paste

about 225 g/8 oz grated
cheese, such as Cheddar,
mozzarella, Asiago or
Mexican queso oaxaco –
one type or a combination

225 ml/8 fl oz chicken or
vegetable stock

5 spring onions, thinly sliced

2–3 tbsp chopped fresh
coriander

handful of romaine lettuce
leaves, shredded

1 avocado, pitted, peeled,
diced and tossed in
lime juice

4 tbsp soured cream

salsa of your choice

method

Heat the tortillas in a lightly oiled non-stick frying pan;
wrap in foil or a clean tea towel as you work to keep
them warm.

Dip the tortillas into the mole sauce and pile up on a
plate. Fill the inside of the top sauced tortilla with a few
spoonfuls of grated cheese. Roll up and arrange in a
shallow ovenproof dish. Repeat with the remaining
tortillas, reserving a handful of the cheese to sprinkle
over the top.

Pour the rest of the mole sauce over the rolled tortillas,
then pour the stock over the top. Sprinkle with the
reserved cheese and cover with foil.

Bake in a preheated oven, 190°C/375°F/Gas Mark 5, for
20 minutes, or until the tortillas are piping hot and the
cheese filling melts.

Arrange the spring onions, coriander, lettuce, avocado and
soured cream on top. Add salsa to taste. Serve at once.

jalisco-style eggs

ingredients

SERVES 4

4 soft corn tortillas

1 avocado

lime or lemon juice, for tossing

175 g/6 oz fresh chorizo
   sausage, sliced or diced

2 tbsp butter or water,
   for cooking

4 eggs

4 tbsp crumbled feta cheese

salsa of your choice

1 tbsp chopped fresh
   coriander

1 tbsp finely chopped spring
   onions

method

Heat the tortillas in an unoiled non-stick frying pan,
sprinkling them with a few drops of water as they heat;
wrap the tortillas in foil or a clean tea towel as you work
to keep them warm. Alternatively, heat through in a
stack in the frying pan, moving the tortillas from the top
to the bottom so that they warm evenly. Wrap to keep
them warm.

Cut the avocado in half around the stone. Twist apart,
then remove the stone with a knife. Carefully peel off the
skin, dice the flesh and toss in lime juice to prevent
discoloration.

Heat a separate frying pan, add the chorizo and cook
until browned, then arrange on each warmed tortilla.
Keep warm.

Meanwhile, heat the butter or water in the non-stick
frying pan, break in an egg and cook until the white is set
but the yolk is still soft. Remove from the pan and place
on top of one tortilla. Keep warm. Cook the remaining
eggs in the same way, adding to the tortillas.

Arrange the avocado, cheese and a spoonful of salsa
on each tortilla. Add the coriander and spring onions
and serve.

huevos rancheros

ingredients

SERVES 4

2 tbsp butter, bacon fat or lard

2 onions, finely chopped

2 garlic cloves, finely chopped

2 red or yellow peppers,
deseeded and diced

2 fresh mild green chillies,
deseeded and finely
chopped

4 large ripe tomatoes, peeled
and chopped

2 tbsp lemon or lime juice

2 tsp dried oregano

salt and pepper

4 large eggs

85 g/3 oz Cheddar cheese,
grated

method

Heat the butter in a heavy-based frying pan over medium heat. Add the onions and garlic and cook, stirring frequently, for 5 minutes, or until softened. Add the peppers and chillies and cook for 5 minutes, until softened.

Add the tomatoes, lemon juice and oregano and season to taste with salt and pepper. Bring to the boil, then reduce the heat, cover and simmer for 10 minutes, or until thickened, adding a little more lemon juice if the mixture becomes too dry.

Transfer the mixture to a large, ovenproof dish. Make 4 hollows in the mixture and break an egg into each. Bake in a preheated oven, 180°C/350°F/Gas Mark 4, for 12–15 minutes, or until the eggs are set.

Sprinkle with grated cheese and return to the oven for 3–4 minutes, or until the cheese has melted. Serve at once.

eggs oaxaca-style

ingredients

SERVES 4

1 kg/2 lb 4 oz ripe tomatoes
about 12 button onions,
    halved
8 garlic cloves, whole and
    unpeeled
2 fresh mild green chillies
pinch of ground cumin
pinch of dried oregano
salt and pepper
pinch of sugar (optional)
2–3 tsp vegetable oil
8 eggs, lightly beaten
1–2 tbsp tomato purée
1–2 tbsp chopped fresh
    coriander, to garnish

method

Heat an unoiled heavy-based frying pan. Add the
tomatoes and char lightly, turning them once or twice.
Remove from the pan and set aside to cool.

Meanwhile, lightly char the onions, garlic and chillies in
the pan. Remove from the pan and let cool slightly.

Cut the cooled tomatoes into pieces and place in a food
processor or blender with their charred skins. Remove
the stalks and seeds from the chillies, then peel and
chop. Remove the skins from the garlic, then chop.
Coarsely chop the onions. Add the chopped chillies, garlic
and onions to the tomatoes.

Process to make a coarse purée, then add the cumin
and oregano. Season to taste with salt and pepper and
add sugar, if necessary.

Heat the oil in a non-stick frying pan. Add a ladleful of
egg and cook to make a thin omelette. Continue to make
omelettes, stacking them on a plate as they are cooked.
Slice into noodle-like ribbons.

Bring the sauce to the boil in a saucepan and adjust the
seasoning, adding tomato purée to taste. Add the omelette
strips, warm through, then serve at once, garnished with
a sprinkling of coriander.

made with meat

National cuisine is all about making creative use of the local produce, and Mexico is no exception. Beef, pork and chicken are all used, avocados make frequent appearances, and then there is tequila, the now world-famous local liquor that is excellent as a meat tenderizer. And chocolate … not in every recipe, of course, but it seems that meat and chocolate marry remarkably well, so do be adventurous and try adding a little to a steak chilli, or make the Chicken Mole Poblano illustrated here.

In Mexico the main meal is traditionally served at midday and is a gloriously relaxed affair, usually with a meat or fish dish for the central course. Meat dishes are often cooked very slowly, either as a stew or in the oven, as a casserole. And virtually every dish will contain the ingredient that, along with tortillas and beans, defines Mexican food – chillies. They are eaten raw and cooked, sliced and stewed, stuffed and puréed, soaked and fried, and appear at every meal to add flavour, texture, colour and aroma. Some recipes call for nothing more than a hint of mild chilli powder, while two of the fresh version of the milder chillies – anaheim and poblano – are perfect for stuffing. Other recipes use chillies that start hot and get hotter, so be warned – they are fire for your tastebuds!

steak, avocado & bean salad

ingredients

SERVES 4–6

350 g/12 oz tender steak,
    such as sirloin

4 garlic cloves, chopped

juice of 1 lime

4 tbsp extra-virgin olive oil

salt and pepper

1 tbsp white or red wine vinegar

¼ tsp mild chilli powder

¼ tsp ground cumin

½ tsp paprika

5 spring onions, thinly sliced

about 200 g/7 oz crisp lettuce
    leaves, such as romaine

225 g/8 oz canned sweetcorn
    kernels, drained

400 g/14 oz canned pinto,
    black or red kidney beans,
    drained

1 avocado, peeled, sliced and
    tossed with lime juice

2 ripe tomatoes, diced

¼ fresh green or red chilli,
    chopped

3 tbsp chopped fresh
    coriander

generous handful of crisp tortilla
    chips, broken into pieces

method

Place the steak in a non-metallic dish with the garlic and half the lime juice and oil. Season to taste with salt and pepper, cover and marinate for 30 minutes.

To make the dressing, combine the remaining lime juice and oil with the vinegar, chilli powder, cumin and paprika in a small non-metallic bowl, then set aside.

Pan-fry the steak, or cook under a preheated very hot grill, until browned on the outside and cooked to your liking in the middle. Transfer to a board, cut into strips, and reserve; keep warm or let cool.

Toss the spring onions with the lettuce and arrange on a serving platter. Pour half the dressing over the leaves, then arrange the sweetcorn, beans, avocado and tomatoes over the top. Sprinkle with the chilli and coriander.

Arrange the steak and the tortilla chips on top, pour over the rest of the dressing and serve at once.

tequila-marinated beef steaks

ingredients

SERVES 4

2 tbsp olive oil

3 tbsp tequila

3 tbsp freshly squeezed
orange juice

1 tbsp freshly squeezed
lime juice

3 garlic cloves, crushed

2 tsp chilli powder

2 tsp ground cumin

1 tsp dried oregano

salt and pepper

4 sirloin steaks

method

Place the oil, tequila, orange and lime juices, garlic, chilli powder, cumin, oregano and salt and pepper to taste in a large, shallow, non-metallic dish and mix together. Add the steaks and turn to coat in the marinade. Cover and chill in the refrigerator for at least 2 hours or overnight, turning occasionally.

Preheat the barbecue and oil the rack. Let the steaks return to room temperature, then remove from the marinade. Cook over hot coals for 3–4 minutes on each side for medium, or longer according to taste, basting frequently with the marinade. Serve at once.

michoacan beef

ingredients

SERVES 4

about 3 tbsp plain flour

salt and pepper

1 kg/2 lb 4 oz stewing beef, cut
    into large bite-size pieces

2 tbsp vegetable oil

2 onions, chopped

5 garlic cloves, chopped

400 g/14 oz tomatoes, diced

1$^{1}/_{2}$ dried chipotle chillies,
    reconstituted, deseeded
    and cut into thin strips, or
    a few shakes of bottled
    chipotle salsa

1.5 litres/48 fl oz beef stock

350 g/12 oz green beans

pinch of sugar

to serve

simmered beans

freshly cooked rice

method

Place the flour in a large bowl and season to taste with salt
and pepper. Add the beef and toss to coat well. Remove
the beef from the bowl, shaking off the excess flour.

Heat the oil in a frying pan. Add the beef and brown
briefly over high heat. Reduce the heat to medium, add
the onions and garlic and cook for 2 minutes.

Add the tomatoes, chillies and stock, then cover and
simmer over low heat for 1$^{1}/_{2}$ hours, or until the meat is
very tender, adding the green beans and sugar 15 minutes
before the end of the cooking time. Skim off any fat that
rises to the surface every now and again.

Transfer to individual bowls and serve with simmered
beans and rice.

lone star chilli

ingredients

SERVES 4

1 tbsp cumin seeds

650 g/1 lb 7 oz rump steak,
    cut into 2.5-cm/1-inch
    cubes

plain flour, well seasoned with
    salt and pepper, for
    coating

3 tbsp beef drippings, bacon
    fat or vegetable oil

2 onions, finely chopped

4 garlic cloves, finely chopped

1 tbsp dried oregano

2 tsp paprika

4 dried red chillies, such as
    ancho or pasilla, crushed,
    or to taste

1 large bottle of South
    American lager

115 g/4 oz plain chocolate

method

Dry-fry the cumin seeds in a heavy-based frying pan over medium heat, shaking the pan, for 3–4 minutes, or until lightly toasted. Let cool, then grind in a mortar with a pestle. Alternatively, use a coffee grinder reserved for the purpose.

Toss the beef in the seasoned flour to coat. Melt the fat in a large, heavy-based saucepan. Add the beef, in batches, and cook until browned on all sides. Remove the beef with a slotted spoon and set aside.

Add the onions and garlic to the pan and cook gently for 5 minutes, or until softened. Add the cumin, oregano, paprika and chillies and cook, stirring, for 2 minutes. Return the beef to the pan, pour over most of the lager, then add the chocolate. Bring to the boil, stirring, then reduce the heat, cover and simmer for 2–3 hours, or until the beef is very tender, adding more lager if necessary.

chillies stuffed with beef

ingredients

SERVES 4

4 large fresh poblano chillies

plain flour, for dusting

vegetable oil, for frying

spicy beef filling

500 g/1 lb 2 oz minced beef

1 onion, finely chopped

3 garlic cloves, finely chopped

4 tbsp dry or sweet sherry

pinch of ground cinnamon

pinch of ground cloves

pinch of ground cumin

salt and pepper

400 g/14 oz canned chopped
   tomatoes

1–3 tsp sugar

1 tbsp vinegar

3 tbsp chopped fresh coriander

2–3 tbsp coarsely chopped
   toasted almonds

Quick Tomato Sauce (see
   page 162), to serve

batter

3 eggs, separated

6–8 tbsp plain flour

pinch of salt

125 ml/4 fl oz water

method

Preheat the grill to medium. Roast the chillies under the hot grill until the skin is charred. Place in a plastic bag, twist to seal well and let stand for 20 minutes. Make a slit in the side of each chilli and remove the seeds, leaving the stalks intact. Set aside.

To make the filling, brown the meat and onion together in a heavy-based frying pan over medium heat. Pour off any extra fat, then add the garlic and sherry and boil down until the liquid has nearly evaporated.

Add the cinnamon, cloves, cumin and salt and pepper to taste. Stir in the tomatoes, sugar and vinegar and cook over medium heat until the tomatoes have reduced to a thick, strongly flavoured sauce.

Stir in the coriander and almonds and heat through. Stuff as much of the filling into the chillies as will fit, then dust each with flour. Set aside.

To make the batter, lightly beat the egg yolks in a large bowl with the flour, salt and enough of the water to make a thick mixture. In a separate bowl, whisk the egg whites until they form stiff peaks. Fold the egg whites into the batter, then gently dip each stuffed chilli into the batter.

Heat the oil in a deep frying pan until very hot and just smoking. Add the chillies and fry until they are golden brown. Serve hot, topped with the Quick Tomato Sauce.

classic beef fajitas

ingredients

SERVES 4–6

700 g/1 lb 9 oz sirloin steak
or other tender beef steak,
cut into strips

3 garlic cloves, chopped

juice of 1 lime

large pinch of mild chilli
powder

large pinch of paprika

large pinch of ground cumin

1–2 tbsp extra-virgin olive oil

salt and pepper

12 flour tortillas (see page
206)

vegetable oil, for oiling
and frying

1–2 avocados, pitted, peeled,
diced and tossed with
lime juice

125 ml/4 fl oz soured cream

salsa

8 ripe tomatoes, diced

3 spring onions, sliced

1–2 fresh green chillies,
deseeded and chopped

3–4 tbsp chopped fresh
coriander

5–8 radishes, diced

ground cumin, to taste

salt and pepper

method

Combine the strips of steak with the garlic, half the lime
juice (toss the avocados in the remaining juice when
ready to serve, see ingredients), the chilli powder,
paprika, cumin and oil. Add salt and pepper to taste and
mix well. Cover and marinate for at least 30 minutes at
room temperature, or overnight in the refrigerator.

To make the pico de gallo salsa, place the tomatoes in
a bowl with the spring onions, chillies, coriander and
radishes. Season to taste with cumin, salt and pepper.
Set aside.

Heat the tortillas in a lightly oiled non-stick frying pan;
wrap in foil or a clean tea towel as you work to keep
them warm.

Heat a little oil in a large frying pan or preheated wok.
Add the beef and stir-fry over high heat until browned
and just cooked through.

Serve the sizzling hot meat with the warmed tortillas, salsa,
avocado and soured cream for each person to make his or
her own rolled-up fajitas.

beef enchiladas

ingredients

SERVES 4

2 tbsp olive oil, plus extra
for oiling

2 large onions, thinly sliced

550 g/1 lb 4 oz lean beef,
cut into bite-size pieces

1 tbsp ground cumin

1–2 tsp cayenne pepper,
or to taste

1 tsp paprika

salt and pepper

8 soft corn tortillas

1 quantity taco sauce
(see page 138)

225 g/8 oz Cheddar cheese,
grated

method

Heat the oil in a large frying pan over low heat. Add the onions and cook for 10 minutes, or until soft and golden. Remove with a slotted spoon and set aside.

Increase the heat to high, add the beef and cook, stirring, for 2–3 minutes, or until browned on all sides. Reduce the heat to medium, add the spices and salt and pepper to taste, and cook, stirring constantly, for 2 minutes.

Warm each tortilla in a lightly oiled non-stick frying pan for 15 seconds on each side, then dip each, in turn, in the sauce. Top with a little of the beef, onions and grated cheese and roll up.

Place seam-side down in an oiled baking dish, top with the remaining sauce and grated cheese, and bake in a preheated oven, 180°C/350°F/Gas Mark 4, for 30 minutes. Serve at once.

ropa vieja

ingredients

SERVES 6

1.5 kg/3 lb 5 oz flank beef
　steak or other stewing meat
beef stock
1 carrot, sliced
10 garlic cloves, sliced
salt and pepper
2 tbsp vegetable oil
2 onions, thinly sliced
3–4 mild fresh green chillies,
　such as Anaheim or
　poblano, deseeded
　and sliced
warmed flour tortillas (see
　page 206), to serve

salad garnishes

3 ripe tomatoes, diced
8–10 radishes, diced
3–4 tbsp chopped fresh
　coriander
4–5 spring onions, chopped
1–2 limes, cut into wedges

method

Place the meat in a large saucepan and cover with a mixture of stock and water. Add the carrot and half the garlic with salt and pepper to taste. Cover and bring to the boil, then reduce the heat to low. Skim the scum that rises to the surface, then re-cover the pan and cook the meat gently for 2 hours, or until very tender.

Remove the pan from the heat and let the meat cool in the liquid. When cool enough to handle, remove from the liquid and shred with your fingers and a fork.

Heat the oil in a large, heavy-based frying pan. Add the remaining garlic, onions and chillies and cook until lightly coloured. Remove from the pan and set aside.

Add the meat to the pan and cook over medium–high heat until browned and crisp. Transfer to a serving dish. Top with the onion mixture and surround with the tomatoes, radishes, coriander, spring onions and lime wedges. Serve with warmed tortillas.

spicy meat & chipotle hash

ingredients

SERVES 6

1 tbsp vegetable oil

1 onion, finely chopped

450 g/1 lb leftover meat, such as simmered pork or beef, cooled and cut into strips

1 tbsp mild chilli powder

2 ripe tomatoes, deseeded and diced

about 250 ml/8 fl oz meat stock

1/2–1 canned chipotle chilli, mashed, plus a little of the marinade, or a few shakes of bottled chipotle salsa

chopped fresh coriander, plus extra to serve

to serve

warmed soft corn tortillas

125 ml/4 fl oz soured cream

4–6 tbsp chopped radishes

3–4 crisp lettuce leaves, such as romaine, shredded

method

Heat the oil in a frying pan. Add the onion and cook until softened, stirring occasionally. Add the meat and cook for about 3 minutes, or until lightly browned, stirring.

Add the chilli powder, tomatoes and stock and cook until the tomatoes reduce to a sauce; mash the meat a little as it cooks.

Add the chilli and continue to cook and mash until the sauce and meat are nearly blended.

Serve the dish, garnished with chopped coriander, with a stack of warmed corn tortillas so that people can fill them with the meaty mixture to make tacos. Also serve soured cream, additional coriander, radishes and lettuce for each person to add to the meat.

meatballs in spicy-sweet sauce

ingredients

SERVES 4

225 g/8 oz minced pork

225 g/8 oz minced beef or lamb

6 tbsp cooked rice or finely crushed tortilla chips

1 egg, lightly beaten

1 1/2 onions, finely chopped

5 garlic cloves, finely chopped

1/2 tsp ground cumin

large pinch of ground cinnamon

2 tbsp raisins

1 tbsp molasses sugar

1–2 tbsp cider or wine vinegar

400 g/14 oz canned tomatoes, drained and chopped

350 ml/12 fl oz beef stock

1–2 tbsp mild chilli or ancho chilli powder

1 tbsp paprika

1 tbsp chopped fresh coriander

1 tbsp chopped fresh parsley

2 tbsp vegetable oil

2 sweet potatoes, peeled and cut into small chunks

salt and pepper

grated cheese, to serve

method

Mix the meat thoroughly with the rice or crushed tortilla chips, the egg, half the onion and garlic, the cumin, cinnamon and raisins.

Divide the mixture into even-size pieces and roll into balls. Fry the balls in a non-stick frying pan over medium heat until brown. Remove the balls from the pan and set aside. Wipe the pan clean.

Place the sugar in a food processor or blender with the vinegar, tomatoes, stock, chilli powder, paprika and remaining onion and garlic. Process until blended, then stir in the herbs. Set aside.

Heat the oil in the cleaned frying pan. Add the sweet potatoes and cook until tender and golden brown. Pour in the blended sauce and add the meatballs to the pan. Cook for 10 minutes, or until the meatballs are heated through and the flavours have combined. Season to taste with salt and pepper. Serve with grated cheese.

chilli verde

ingredients

SERVES 4

1 kg/2 lb 4 oz pork, cut into
   bite-size chunks
1 onion, chopped
2 bay leaves
1 whole garlic bulb, cut in half
1 stock cube
2 garlic cloves, chopped
450 g/1 lb fresh tomatillos,
   husks removed, cooked in
   a small amount of water
   until just tender, then
   chopped, or canned
2 large fresh mild green
   chillies, such as Anaheim,
   or 1 green pepper and
   2 jalapeño chillies,
   deseeded and chopped
3 tbsp vegetable oil
225 ml/8 fl oz pork or chicken
   stock
1/2 tsp mild chilli powder, such
   as ancho or New Mexico
1/2 tsp ground cumin
4–6 tbsp chopped fresh
   coriander, to garnish

to serve

warmed flour tortillas (see
   page 206)
lime wedges

method

Place the pork in a large, flameproof casserole with the onion, bay leaves and garlic bulb. Add water to cover and the stock cube and bring to the boil. Skim off the scum that rises to the surface, reduce the heat to very low and simmer gently for 1 1/2 hours, or until the meat is very tender.

Meanwhile, place the chopped garlic in a food processor or blender with the tomatillos, chillies and green pepper, if using. Process to a purée.

Heat the oil in a deep frying pan. Add the tomatillo mixture and cook over medium–high heat for 10 minutes, or until thickened. Add the stock, chilli powder and cumin.

When the meat is tender, remove from the casserole and add to the sauce. Simmer gently for 20 minutes, or until the flavours are combined.

Garnish with the chopped coriander and serve with warmed tortillas and lime wedges.

mole of pork & red chillies

ingredients

SERVES 6

1.25 kg/2 lb 12 oz pork shoulder or lean belly, cut into bite-size pieces

1 onion, chopped

1 whole garlic bulb

2 bay leaves

salt and pepper

1–2 stock cubes

6 dried ancho chillies

6 guajillo or de agua chillies

3–5 large ripe flavourful tomatoes

1/4 tsp ground cloves

1/4 tsp ground allspice

85 g/3 oz sesame seeds, toasted

1 large ripe plantain or banana, peeled and diced

3 tbsp vegetable oil

6–8 waxy potatoes, cut into chunks

3 tbsp yerba santa or, if unavailable, a combination of chopped fresh mint, oregano and coriander, plus a sprig to garnish

1 cinnamon stick

method

Place the pork in a large flameproof casserole with the onion, garlic, bay leaves and salt and pepper to taste. Fill with cold water to the top. Bring to the boil, then reduce the heat to a slow simmer. Skim off the scum that rises to the surface, then stir in the stock cubes. Cook, covered, for 3 hours, or until the pork is very tender.

Meanwhile, lightly roast the chillies in an unoiled heavy-based frying pan until they just change colour. Place them in a heatproof bowl and cover with boiling water. Cover and set aside to soften for 20–30 minutes.

Preheat the grill to medium. Roast the tomatoes in the frying pan to brown the bottoms, then char the tops under the hot grill. Let cool.

When the chillies are softened, remove the stalks and seeds, transfer to a food processor or blender and process with enough liquid to form a paste. Add the roasted tomatoes, cloves, allspice, two-thirds of the sesame seeds and the plantain and process until smooth.

Remove the pork from the pan and reserve. Skim the fat from the surface of the stock.

Heat the oil in a separate saucepan. Add the tomato mixture and cook for 10 minutes, or until thickened. Add the potatoes and herbs with enough stock to keep the potatoes covered in sauce. Add the cinnamon stick. Cook, covered, until the potatoes are tender. Add the pork and heat through. Serve in bowls, sprinkled with the remaining sesame seeds.

spicy pork & vegetable hotpot

ingredients

SERVES 4

plain flour, for coating

450 g/1 lb boneless pork, cut into 2.5-cm/1-inch cubes

1 tbsp vegetable oil

225 g/8 oz chorizo sausage, outer casing removed, cut into bite-size chunks

1 onion, coarsely chopped

4 garlic cloves, finely chopped

2 celery stalks, chopped

1 cinnamon stick, broken

2 bay leaves

2 tsp allspice

2 carrots, sliced

2–3 fresh red chillies, deseeded and finely chopped

6 ripe tomatoes, peeled and chopped

1 litre/32 fl oz pork or vegetable stock

2 sweet potatoes, cut into chunks

corn kernels, cut from 1 ear fresh sweetcorn

1 tbsp chopped fresh oregano

salt and pepper

fresh oregano, to garnish

method

Season the flour well with salt and pepper and toss the pork in it to coat. Heat the oil in a large, heavy-based saucepan or ovenproof casserole. Add the chorizo and lightly brown on all sides. Remove the chorizo with a slotted spoon and set aside.

Add the pork, in batches, and cook until browned on all sides. Remove the pork with a slotted spoon and set aside. Add the onion, garlic and celery to the pan and cook for 5 minutes, or until softened.

Add the cinnamon, bay leaves and allspice and cook, stirring, for 2 minutes. Add the pork, carrots, chillies, tomatoes and stock. Bring to the boil, then reduce the heat, cover and simmer for 1 hour, or until the pork is tender.

Return the chorizo to the pan with the sweet potatoes, corn, oregano and salt and pepper to taste. Cover and simmer for a further 30 minutes, or until the vegetables are tender. Serve garnished with oregano.

carnitas

ingredients

SERVES 4–6

1 kg/2 lb 4 oz pork,
   such as lean belly
1 onion, chopped
1 whole garlic bulb,
   cut in half
1/2 tsp ground cumin
2 meat stock cubes
2 bay leaves
salt and pepper
fresh chilli strips, to garnish

to serve

freshly cooked rice
refried beans (see page 202)
   or canned
salsa of your choice

method

Place the pork in a heavy-based saucepan with the onion, garlic, cumin, stock cubes and bay leaves. Add water to cover. Bring to the boil, then reduce the heat to very low. Skim off the scum that rises to the surface. Continue to cook very gently for 2 hours, or until the pork is tender. Remove from the heat and let the pork cool in the liquid.

Remove the pork from the pan with a slotted spoon. Cut off any skin (roast separately to make crackling). Cut the pork into bite-size pieces and sprinkle with salt and pepper to taste. Reserve 300 ml/10 fl oz of the cooking liquid.

Brown the pork in a heavy-based frying pan for 15 minutes, to cook out the fat. Add the reserved cooking liquid and allow to reduce down. Continue to cook the meat for 15 minutes, covering the pan to avoid splattering. Turn the pork every now and again.

Transfer the pork to a serving dish, garnish with chilli strips and serve with rice, refried beans and salsa.

spicy pork with prunes

ingredients

SERVES 4–6

1 pork joint, such as leg
    or shoulder, weighing
    1.5 kg/3 lb 5 oz
juice of 2–3 limes
10 garlic cloves, chopped
3–4 tbsp mild chilli powder,
    such as ancho or
    New Mexico
4 tbsp vegetable oil
salt
2 onions, chopped
550 ml/18 fl oz chicken stock
25 small tart tomatoes,
    coarsely chopped
25 prunes, pitted
1–2 tsp sugar
pinch of ground cinnamon
pinch of ground allspice
pinch of ground cumin
warmed corn tortillas, to serve

method

Combine the pork with the lime juice, garlic, chilli powder, half the oil and salt to taste in a non-metallic bowl. Cover and marinate in the refrigerator overnight.

Remove the pork from the marinade. Wipe the pork dry with kitchen paper and reserve the marinade. Heat the remaining oil in a flameproof casserole and brown the pork evenly until just golden. Add the onions, the reserved marinade and stock. Cover and cook in a preheated oven, 180°C/350°F/Gas Mark 4, for 2–3 hours, or until tender.

Remove the casserole from the oven and spoon off the fat from the surface of the cooking liquid. Add the tomatoes. Return to the oven for 20 minutes, or until the tomatoes are tender. Remove the casserole from the oven. Mash the tomatoes into a coarse purée. Add the prunes and sugar, then adjust the seasoning, adding cinnamon, allspice and cumin, as well as extra chilli powder, if wished.

Increase the oven temperature to 200°C/400°F/Gas Mark 6, and return the casserole to the oven for a further 20–30 minutes, or until the meat has browned on top and the juices have thickened.

Remove the meat from the casserole and let stand for a few minutes. Carefully carve the joint into thin slices and spoon the sauce over the top. Serve warm, with corn tortillas.

pork tostadas

ingredients

SERVES 6–8

1 tbsp vegetable oil, plus
    extra for cooking
1 small onion, finely chopped
2 garlic cloves, finely chopped
450 g/1 lb fresh minced pork
2 tsp ground cumin
2 tsp chilli powder, plus
    extra to garnish
1 tsp ground cinnamon
salt and pepper
6 soft corn tortillas,
    cut into wedges

to serve

shredded iceberg lettuce
soured cream
finely diced red pepper

method

Heat the 1 tablespoon of oil in a heavy-based frying pan
over medium heat. Add the onion and garlic and cook,
stirring frequently, for 5 minutes, or until softened.
Increase the heat, add the minced pork and cook,
stirring constantly to break up any lumps, until
well browned.

Add the cumin, chilli powder, cinnamon and salt
and pepper to taste and cook, stirring, for 2 minutes.
Cover and cook over low heat, stirring occasionally,
for 10 minutes.

Meanwhile, heat a little oil in a non-stick frying pan. Add
the tortilla wedges, in batches, and cook on both sides
until crisp. Drain on kitchen paper.

Transfer to a serving plate and top with the pork mixture,
followed by the lettuce, a little soured cream and diced
pepper. Garnish with a sprinkling of chilli powder and
serve at once.

pork quesadillas with pinto beans

ingredients

SERVES 4

1 quantity carnitas (see
    page 84) or about 100 g/
    3^1/$_2$ oz cooked pork strips
    per person

1 ripe tomato, deseeded
    and diced

^{1}/$_2$ onion, chopped

3 tbsp chopped fresh
    coriander

4 large flour tortillas

350 g/12 oz grated or thinly
    sliced cheese, such as
    mozzarella or Swiss

about 375 g/13^1/$_2$ oz cooked
    drained pinto beans

hot salsa of your choice or
    bottled hot sauce, to taste

pickled jalapeño chillies, cut
    into thin rings, to taste

vegetable oil, for frying

to serve

pickled chillies
mixed salad

method

Heat the carnitas in a pan and keep hot over low heat.

Combine the tomato, onion and coriander in a bowl and
set aside.

Heat a tortilla in an unoiled non-stick frying pan.
Sprinkle the tortilla with cheese, then top with some of the
meat, beans and reserved tomato mixture. Add salsa and
chilli rings to taste. Fold over the sides of the tortilla to make
a pocket.

Heat the pockets gently on each side in the frying pan,
adding a few drops of oil to keep it all supple and
succulent, until the tortilla is golden and the cheese inside
has melted. Keep warm. Repeat with the remaining
tortillas and filling.

Transfer the quesadillas to a plate and serve at once with
pickled chillies and salad.

chorizo & cheese quesadillas

ingredients

SERVES 4

115 g/4 oz mozzarella
 cheese, grated

115 g/4 oz Cheddar cheese,
 grated

225 g/8 oz cooked chorizo
 sausage, outer casing
 removed, or ham, diced

4 spring onions, finely
 chopped

2 fresh green chillies, such
 as poblano, deseeded and
 finely chopped

salt and pepper

8 flour tortillas (see page 206)

vegetable oil, for brushing

lime wedges, to garnish

method

Place the cheeses, chorizo, spring onions, chillies and
salt and pepper to taste in a bowl and mix together.

Divide the mixture between 4 flour tortillas, then top with
the remaining tortillas.

Brush a large, non-stick or heavy-based frying pan with
oil and heat over medium heat. Add 1 quesadilla and
cook, pressing it down with a spatula, for 4–5 minutes,
or until the underside is crisp and lightly browned. Turn
over and cook the other side until the cheese is melting.
Remove from the pan and keep warm. Cook the
remaining quesadillas individually.

Cut each quesadilla into quarters, arrange on a warmed
serving plate and serve, garnished with lime wedges.

burritos of lamb
& black beans

ingredients

SERVES 4

650 g/1 lb 7 oz lean lamb
3 garlic cloves, finely chopped
juice of $1/2$ lime
$1/2$ tsp mild chilli powder
$1/2$ tsp ground cumin
large pinch of dried oregano
    leaves, crushed
1–2 tbsp extra-virgin olive oil
salt and pepper
400 g/14 oz cooked black
    beans, seasoned with a little
    cumin, salt and pepper
4 large flour tortillas
2–3 tbsp chopped fresh
    coriander, plus a few
    sprigs to garnish
salsa, preferably chipotle salsa
    (see page 164)
lime wedges, to serve
    (optional)

method

Slice the lamb into thin strips, then combine with the garlic, lime juice, chilli powder, cumin, oregano and oil in a non-metallic bowl. Season with salt and pepper, cover and marinate in the refrigerator for 4 hours.

Warm the black beans with a little water in a saucepan.

Heat the tortillas in an unoiled non-stick frying pan, sprinkling them with a few drops of water as they heat; wrap the tortillas in foil or a clean tea towel as you work to keep them warm. Alternatively, heat through in a stack in the frying pan, moving the tortillas from the top to the bottom so that they warm evenly. Wrap to keep warm.

Stir-fry the lamb in a heavy-based non-stick frying pan over high heat until browned on all sides. Remove the pan from the heat.

Spoon some of the beans and browned meat into a tortilla, sprinkle with coriander, then add a little salsa and fold in the sides. Repeat with the remaining tortillas. Garnish with coriander sprigs and serve at once with lime wedges and any spare salsa, if wished.

turkey with mole

ingredients

SERVES 4

4 turkey portions, each cut
    into 4 pieces
about 500 ml/16 fl oz chicken
    stock, plus extra for
    thinning
about 250 ml/8 fl oz water
1 onion, chopped
1 whole garlic bulb, divided
    into cloves and peeled
1 celery stalk, chopped
1 bay leaf
1 bunch fresh coriander,
    finely chopped
575 ml/18 fl oz mole poblano
    (see page 158) or use
    ready-made mole paste,
    thinned as instructed on
    the container
4–5 tbsp sesame seeds,
    to garnish

method

Arrange the turkey in a large flameproof casserole.
Pour the stock and water around the turkey, then add
the onion, garlic, celery, bay leaf and half the coriander.

Cover and bake in a preheated oven, 190°C/375°F/Gas
Mark 5, for 1–1$\frac{1}{2}$ hours, or until the turkey is very tender.
Add extra liquid if needed.

Warm the mole sauce in a saucepan with enough stock
to make it the consistency of thin cream.

To toast the sesame seeds for the garnish, place the seeds
in an unoiled frying pan and dry-fry, shaking the pan,
until lightly golden.

Arrange the turkey pieces on a serving plate and spoon
the warmed mole sauce over the top. Sprinkle with the
toasted sesame seeds and the remaining chopped
coriander and serve.

chicken with yucatan vinegar sauce

ingredients

SERVES 4–6

8 small boned chicken thighs

chicken stock

15–20 garlic cloves, unpeeled

1 tsp coarsely ground black
    pepper

1/2 tsp ground cloves

2 tsp crumbled dried oregano
    or 1/2 tsp crushed bay leaves

about 1/2 tsp salt

1 tbsp lime juice

1 tsp cumin seeds, lightly
    toasted

1 tbsp plain flour, plus extra
    for dredging

125 ml/4 fl oz vegetable oil

3–4 onions, thinly sliced

2 fresh chillies, preferably
    mild yellow ones, such as
    Mexican Guero or similar
    Turkish or Greek chillies,
    deseeded and sliced

100 ml/3 1/2 fl oz cider or
    sherry vinegar

method

Place the chicken in a saucepan with enough stock
to cover. Bring to the boil, then reduce the heat and
simmer for 5 minutes. Remove from the heat and let the
chicken continue to cook while cooling in the stock.

Meanwhile, roast the garlic in an unoiled heavy-based,
non-stick frying pan until the cloves are lightly browned
on all sides and tender inside. Remove from the heat.
When cool enough to handle, squeeze the flesh from the
skins and place in a bowl.

Using a pestle and mortar, grind the garlic with the pepper,
cloves, oregano, salt, lime juice and three-quarters of the
cumin seeds. Mix with the flour.

Remove the chicken from the stock, reserving the stock,
and pat dry. Rub with two-thirds of the spice paste. Cover
and let stand at room temperature for at least 30 minutes
or overnight in the refrigerator.

Heat a little of the oil in a frying pan and cook the onions
and chillies until golden and softened. Pour in the vinegar
and remaining cumin seeds, cook for a few minutes,
then add the reserved stock and remaining spice paste.
Boil, stirring, for 10 minutes, or until reduced in volume.

Dredge the chicken in flour. Heat the remaining oil
in a heavy-based frying pan. Fry the chicken until lightly
browned and the juices run clear when a skewer is
inserted into the thickest part. Serve topped with
the sauce.

chicken mole poblano

ingredients

SERVES 4

3 tbsp olive oil

4 chicken pieces, about
175 g/6 oz each, halved

1 onion, chopped

2 garlic cloves, finely chopped

1 hot dried red chilli, such as
chipotle, or 2 milder dried
chillies, such as ancho,
reconstituted and finely
chopped

1 tbsp sesame seeds, toasted,
plus extra to garnish

1 tbsp chopped almonds

1/4 tsp each of ground
cinnamon, cumin and
cloves

3 tomatoes, peeled and
chopped

2 tbsp raisins

350 ml/12 fl oz chicken stock

1 tbsp peanut butter

25 g/1 oz plain chocolate with
a high cocoa content,
grated, plus extra to
garnish

salt and pepper

method

Heat 2 tablespoons of the oil in a large frying pan.
Add the chicken and cook until browned on all sides.
Remove the chicken pieces with a slotted spoon and
set aside.

Add the onion, garlic and chillies and cook for 5 minutes,
or until softened. Add the sesame seeds, almonds and
spices and cook, stirring, for 2 minutes. Add the tomatoes,
raisins, stock, peanut butter and chocolate and stir well.
Season to taste with salt and pepper and simmer for
5 minutes.

Transfer the mixture to a food processor or blender and
process until smooth (you may need to do this in batches).

Return the mixture to the frying pan, add the chicken
and bring to the boil. Reduce the heat, cover and
simmer for 1 hour, or until the chicken is very tender,
adding more liquid if necessary.

Serve garnished with sesame seeds and a little grated
chocolate.

tequila-marinated crisp chicken wings

ingredients

SERVES 4

900 g/2 lb chicken wings

11 garlic cloves, finely chopped

juice of 2 limes

juice of 1 orange

2 tbsp tequila

1 tbsp mild chilli powder

2 tsp chipotle salsa
   (see page 164) or
   2 dried chipotle chillies,
   reconstituted and puréed

2 tbsp vegetable oil

1 tsp sugar

1/4 tsp ground allspice

pinch of ground cinnamon

pinch of ground cumin

pinch of dried oregano

barbecued or grilled tomato
   halves, to serve (optional)

method

Cut the chicken wings into 2 pieces at the joint.

Place the chicken wings in a non-metallic dish and add the remaining ingredients. Toss well to coat, then cover and marinate in the refrigerator for at least 3 hours or overnight.

Preheat the barbecue. Cook the chicken wings over the hot coals for 15–20 minutes, or until crisply browned and the juices run clear when a skewer is inserted into the thickest part of the meat, turning occasionally. Alternatively, cook in a ridged griddle pan. Serve at once, with barbecued or grilled tomato halves, if wished.

green chilli &
chicken chilaquiles

ingredients

SERVES 4–6

12 stale tortillas, cut into strips

1 tbsp vegetable oil

1 small cooked chicken, meat
    removed from the bones
    and cut into bite-size pieces

salsa verde

3 tbsp chopped fresh
    coriander

1 tsp finely chopped fresh
    oregano or thyme

4 garlic cloves, finely chopped

1/4 tsp ground cumin

350 g/12 oz grated Cheddar,
    manchego or
    mozzarella cheese

500 ml/16 fl oz chicken stock

115 g/4 oz freshly grated
    Parmesan cheese

to serve

350 ml/12 fl oz soured cream

3–5 spring onions, thinly
    sliced

pickled chillies

method

Place the tortilla strips in a roasting pan, toss with the oil
and bake in a preheated oven, 190°C/375°F/Gas Mark
5, for 30 minutes, or until they are crisp and golden.

Arrange the chicken in a 23- x 33-cm/9- x 13-inch
flameproof casserole, then sprinkle with half the salsa,
coriander, oregano, garlic and cumin and some of the
Cheddar, manchego or mozzarella cheese. Repeat these
layers and top with the tortilla strips.

Pour the stock over the top, then sprinkle with the
remaining cheese. Bake in the oven at the same
temperature for 30 minutes, or until heated through and
the cheese is lightly golden in areas.

Serve with a spoonful of soured cream, sliced spring
onions and pickled chillies to taste.

chicken tostadas with green salsa & chipotle

ingredients

SERVES 4–6

6 soft corn tortillas

vegetable oil, for frying

450 g/1 lb skinned, boned
chicken breast or thigh, cut
into strips or small pieces

250 ml/8 fl oz chicken stock

2 garlic cloves, finely chopped

400 g/14 oz refried beans
(see page 202) or canned

large pinch of ground cumin

225 g/8 oz grated cheese

1 tbsp chopped fresh
coriander

2 ripe tomatoes, diced

handful of crisp lettuce leaves,
such as romaine, shredded

4–6 radishes, diced

3 spring onions, thinly sliced

1 ripe avocado, pitted,
peeled, diced or sliced
and tossed with lime juice

soured cream, to taste

1–2 canned chipotle chillies
in adobo marinade

method

To make the tostadas, fry the tortillas in a small amount
of oil in a non-stick frying pan until crisp. Set aside.

Place the chicken in a saucepan with the stock and garlic.
Bring to the boil, then reduce the heat and cook for 1–2
minutes, or until the chicken begins to turn opaque.

Remove the chicken from the heat and let stand in its
hot liquid to cook through.

Heat the beans in a separate saucepan with enough
water to form a smooth purée. Stir in the cumin and
keep warm.

Reheat the tostadas under a preheated medium grill, if
necessary. Spread the hot beans on the tostadas, then
sprinkle with the cheese. Lift the cooked chicken from
the liquid and divide between the tostadas. Top with the
coriander, tomatoes, lettuce, radishes, spring onions,
avocado, soured cream and a few strips of chipotle.
Serve immediately.

chicken fajitas

ingredients

SERVES 4

3 tbsp olive oil, plus
     extra for drizzling
3 tbsp maple syrup or honey
1 tbsp red wine vinegar
2 garlic cloves, crushed
2 tsp dried oregano
1–2 tsp dried red pepper flakes
salt and pepper
4 skinless, boneless chicken
     breasts
2 red peppers, deseeded and
     cut into 2.5-cm/1-inch
     strips
8 flour tortillas (see page
     206), warmed

method

Place the oil, maple syrup, vinegar, garlic, oregano, pepper flakes and salt and pepper to taste in a large, shallow dish or bowl and mix together.

Slice the chicken across the grain into 2.5-cm/1-inch thick slices. Toss in the marinade until well coated. Cover and chill in the refrigerator for 2–3 hours, turning occasionally.

Heat a griddle pan until hot. Lift the chicken slices from the marinade with a slotted spoon, lay on the griddle pan and cook over medium–high heat for 3–4 minutes on each side, or until cooked through. Remove the chicken to a warmed serving plate and keep warm.

Add the peppers, skin-side down, to the griddle pan and cook for 2 minutes on each side. Transfer to the serving plate.

Serve at once with the warmed tortillas to be used as wraps.

chicken tacos from puebla

ingredients

SERVES 4

8 soft corn tortillas
2 tsp vegetable oil
225–350 g/8–12 oz leftover
    cooked chicken, diced or
    shredded
salt and pepper
225 g/8 oz canned refried
    beans, warmed with
    2 tbsp water to thin
1/4 tsp ground cumin
1/4 tsp dried oregano
1 avocado, pitted, peeled,
    sliced and tossed with
    lime juice
salsa of your choice
1 canned chipotle chilli in
    adobo marinade, chopped,
    or bottled chipotle salsa
175 ml/6 fl oz soured cream
1/2 onion, chopped
handful of lettuce leaves
5 radishes, diced

method

Heat the tortillas through in an unoiled non-stick frying pan in a stack, alternating the tortillas from the top to the bottom so that they warm evenly. Wrap in foil or a clean tea towel to keep them warm.

Heat the oil in a frying pan. Add the chicken and heat through. Season to taste with salt and pepper.

Combine the warmed refried beans with the cumin and oregano.

Spread one tortilla with the refried beans, then top with a spoonful of the chicken, a slice or two of avocado, a little salsa, chipotle to taste, a spoonful of soured cream, and a sprinkling of onion, lettuce and radishes. Season to taste with salt and pepper, then roll up as tightly as you can. Repeat with the remaining tortillas and serve at once.

fresh from the sea

The shape of Mexico is defined by its thousands of miles of coastline, and its cuisine is rich in the fruits of the sea – fish and shellfish. Swordfish, salmon, sea bass, red snapper, sole and cod find their way onto the typical Mexican menu, as do squid, prawns, scallops and crab.

As with meat, seafood is given the spicy treatment and chillies add varying degrees of heat to enticing stews, fresh citrus marinades, flavourful pastes for coating the fish, innovative sauces with unusual ingredients like avocado and papaya, luscious fillings for tacos and burritos and tasty toppings for tostadas. Refried beans are used in fish recipes in much the same way as they are in meat dishes – a tostada is quickly made by putting a layer of beans on top of a fried tortilla, adding chunks of poached white fish and finishing with salsa and a spoonful of soured cream.

In some recipes, the fish is served 'cured' rather than cooked – that is, it is left for several hours in a citrus marinade, and the acid from the fruit effectively cooks the flesh. If you are searching for a fish recipe that can be prepared well ahead of time and looks and tastes really impressive, then try the citrus-marinated fish or the ceviche salad at the end of this chapter.

fish with yucatan flavours

ingredients

SERVES 8

4 tbsp annatto seeds, soaked
    in water overnight
3 garlic cloves, finely chopped
1 tbsp mild chilli powder
1 tbsp paprika
1 tsp ground cumin
1/2 tsp dried oregano
2 tbsp beer or tequila
juice of 1 lime and I orange or
    3 tbsp pineapple juice
2 tbsp olive oil
2 tbsp chopped fresh
    coriander
1/4 tsp ground cinnamon
1/4 tsp ground cloves
1 kg/2 lb 4 oz swordfish steaks
banana leaves, for wrapping
    (optional)
fresh coriander sprigs,
    to garnish
orange wedges, to serve

method

Drain the annatto, then crush them to a paste with a pestle and mortar. Work in the garlic, chilli powder, paprika, cumin, oregano, beer, fruit juice, oil, coriander, cinnamon and cloves.

Smear the paste onto the fish, cover and marinate in the refrigerator for at least 3 hours or overnight.

Wrap the fish steaks in banana leaves, tying with string to make pockets. Bring enough water to the boil in a steamer, then add a batch of pockets to the top part of the steamer and steam for 15 minutes, or until the fish is cooked through.

Alternatively, cook the fish without wrapping in the banana leaves. To cook on the barbecue, place in a hinged basket, or on a rack, and cook over hot coals for 5–6 minutes on each side, or until cooked through. Or cook the fish under a preheated hot grill for 5–6 minutes on each side, or until cooked through.

Garnish with coriander sprigs and serve with orange wedges for squeezing over the fish.

spicy grilled salmon

ingredients

SERVES 4

4 salmon steaks, about
175–225 g/6–8 oz each

marinade

4 garlic cloves
2 tbsp extra-virgin olive oil
pinch of ground allspice
pinch of ground cinnamon
juice of 2 limes
1–2 tsp marinade from
canned chipotle chillies or
bottled chipotle chilli salsa
1/4 tsp ground cumin
pinch of sugar
salt and pepper
lime slices, to garnish

to serve

tomato wedges
3 spring onions, finely
chopped
shredded lettuce

method

To make the marinade, finely chop the garlic and place
in a non-metallic bowl with the oil, allspice, cinnamon,
lime juice, chipotle marinade, cumin and sugar. Add salt
and pepper to taste and stir to combine.

Coat the salmon with the garlic mixture, then transfer
to a large non-metallic dish. Cover with clingfilm and
marinate in the refrigerator for 1 hour.

Transfer the salmon to a grill pan and cook under a grill
preheated to medium for 3–4 minutes on each side, or
until cooked through. Alternatively, cook the salmon over
hot coals on a barbecue until cooked through.

To serve, mix the tomato wedges with the spring onions.
Place the salmon on individual plates and arrange the
tomato salad and shredded lettuce alongside. Garnish
with lime slices and serve immediately.

fish baked with lime

ingredients

SERVES 4

1 kg/2 lb 4 oz white fish
    fillets, such as bass,
    flounder or cod

salt and pepper

1 lime, halved

3 tbsp virgin olive oil

1 large onion, finely chopped

3 garlic cloves, finely chopped

2–3 pickled jalapeño chillies,
    chopped, plus extra whole
    chillies to serve (optional)

6–8 tbsp chopped fresh
    coriander

lemon and lime wedges,
    to serve

method

Place the fish fillets in a non-metallic bowl and sprinkle with salt and pepper to taste. Squeeze the juice from the lime over the fish.

Heat the oil in a frying pan. Add the onion and garlic and cook for 2 minutes, or until softened, stirring frequently. Remove from the heat.

Place a third of the onion mixture and a little of the chillies and coriander in the bottom of a shallow baking dish or roasting pan. Arrange the fish on top. Top with the remaining onion mixture, chillies and coriander.

Bake in a preheated oven, 180°C/350°F/Gas Mark 4, for 15–20 minutes, or until the fish has become slightly opaque and firm to the touch. Serve at once, with lemon and lime wedges for squeezing over the fish and whole pickled chillies, if wished.

fish fillets with papaya sauce

ingredients

SERVES 4

4 white fish fillets, such as
sea bass, sole or cod,
about 175 g/6 oz each,
skinned

olive oil, for drizzling

juice of 1 lime

2 tbsp chopped fresh
coriander

salt and pepper

lime wedges, to garnish

papaya sauce

1 large ripe papaya

1 tbsp freshly squeezed
orange juice

1 tbsp freshly squeezed
lime juice

1 tbsp olive oil

1–2 tsp Tabasco sauce

method

Place the fish in a shallow ovenproof dish. Drizzle with oil and squeeze over the lime juice. Sprinkle the chopped coriander over the fish and season with salt and pepper.

Cover the dish tightly with foil and bake in a preheated oven, 180°C/350°F/Gas Mark 4, for 15–20 minutes, or until the fish is just flaking.

Meanwhile, to make the sauce, halve the papaya and scoop out the seeds. Peel the halves and chop the flesh. Place the flesh in a food processor or blender and add the orange and lime juices, oil and Tabasco to taste. Process until smooth.

Transfer the sauce to a pan and heat through gently for 3–4 minutes. Season to taste with salt and pepper.

Serve the fish fillets, in their cooking juices, with the sauce spooned over, garnished with lime wedges.

squid simmered with tomatoes & olives

ingredients

SERVES 4

3 tbsp virgin olive oil

900 g/2 lb cleaned squid, cut
into rings and tentacles

salt and pepper

1 onion, chopped

3 garlic cloves, chopped

400 g/14 oz canned chopped
tomatoes

$^1/_2$–1 fresh mild to medium
green chilli, deseeded and
chopped

1 tbsp finely chopped fresh
parsley

$^1/_4$ tsp chopped fresh thyme

$^1/_4$ tsp chopped fresh oregano

$^1/_4$ tsp chopped fresh
marjoram

large pinch of ground
cinnamon

large pinch of ground allspice

large pinch of sugar

15–20 pimiento-stuffed green
olives, sliced

1 tbsp capers

1 tbsp chopped fresh
coriander, to garnish

method

Heat the oil in a deep, heavy-based frying pan. Add the squid and lightly cook until it turns opaque. Season to taste with salt and pepper and remove from the pan with a slotted spoon. Set aside in a bowl.

Add the onion and garlic to the remaining oil in the skillet and cook for 5 minutes, or until softened. Stir in the tomatoes, chilli, herbs, cinnamon, allspice, sugar and olives. Cover and cook over medium–low heat for 5–10 minutes, or until the mixture thickens slightly. Uncover the pan and cook for a further 5 minutes to concentrate the flavours.

Stir in the reserved squid and any of the juices that have gathered in the bowl. Add the capers and heat through.

Adjust the seasoning, then serve immediately, garnished with coriander.

southwestern seafood stew

ingredients

SERVES 4

1 each of yellow, red and
   orange peppers, deseeded
   and quartered

450 g/1 lb ripe tomatoes

2 large fresh mild green
   chillies, such as poblano

6 garlic cloves, peeled

2 tsp dried oregano or dried
   mixed herbs

2 tbsp olive oil, plus extra for
   drizzling

1 large onion, finely chopped

450 ml/16 fl oz fish, vegetable
   or chicken stock

1 lime, finely grated rind and
   juice of

2 tbsp chopped fresh
   coriander, plus extra to
   garnish

1 bay leaf

salt and pepper

450 g/1 lb red snapper fillets,
   skinned and cut into
   chunks

225 g/8 oz raw prawns,
   shelled and deveined

225 g/8 oz cleaned squid,
   cut into rings

method

Place the pepper quarters, skin side up, in a roasting pan
with the tomatoes, chillies and garlic. Sprinkle with the
dried oregano and drizzle with oil.

Roast in a preheated oven, 200°C/400°F/Gas Mark 4 for
30 minutes, or until the peppers are well browned and
softened.

Remove the roasted vegetables from the oven and set
aside until cool enough to handle. Peel off the skins
from the peppers, tomatoes and chillies and chop the
flesh. Finely chop the garlic.

Heat the oil in a large saucepan. Add the onion and
cook for 5 minutes, or until softened. Add the peppers,
tomatoes, chillies, garlic, stock, lime rind and juice,
chopped coriander, bay leaf and salt and pepper to
taste. Bring to the boil, then stir in the seafood. Reduce
the heat, cover and simmer gently for 10 minutes, or
until the seafood is just cooked through. Garnish with
chopped coriander before serving.

pan-fried scallops mexicana

ingredients

SERVES 4

2 tbsp butter

2 tbsp virgin olive oil

650 g/1 lb 7 oz scallops, shelled

4–5 spring onions, thinly sliced

3–4 garlic cloves, finely chopped

1/2 fresh green chilli, deseeded and finely chopped

2 tbsp finely chopped fresh coriander

1/2 lime

salt and pepper

lime wedges, to serve

method

Heat half the butter and oil in a large, heavy-based frying pan until the butter foams.

Add the scallops and cook quickly until just turning opaque; do not overcook. Remove from the pan with a slotted spoon and keep warm.

Add the remaining butter and oil to the pan, then toss in the spring onions and garlic and cook over medium heat until the spring onions are wilted. Return the scallops to the pan.

Remove the pan from the heat and add the chilli and coriander. Squeeze in the lime juice. Season to taste with salt and pepper and stir to mix well.

Serve immediately with lime wedges for squeezing over the scallops.

prawns in green bean sauce

ingredients

SERVES 4

2 tbsp vegetable oil

3 onions, chopped

5 garlic cloves, chopped

5–7 ripe tomatoes, diced

175–225 g/6–8 oz green beans,
   cut into 5-cm/2-inch pieces
   and blanched for 1 minute

1/4 tsp ground cumin

pinch of ground allspice

pinch of ground cinnamon

1/2–1 canned chipotle chilli in
   adobo marinade, with
   some of the marinade

450 ml/16 fl oz fish stock or
   water mixed with 1 fish
   stock cube

450 g/1 lb raw prawns,
   shelled and deveined

fresh coriander sprigs,
   to garnish

1 lime, cut into wedges,
   to serve (optional)

method

Heat the oil in a large, deep frying pan. Add the onions and garlic and cook over low heat for 5–10 minutes, or until softened. Add the tomatoes and cook for a further 2 minutes.

Add the green beans, cumin, allspice, cinnamon, the chilli and marinade, and stock. Bring to the boil, then reduce the heat and simmer for a few minutes to combine the flavours.

Add the prawns and cook for 1–2 minutes only, then remove the pan from the heat and let the prawns steep in the hot liquid to finish cooking. They are cooked when they have turned a bright pink colour.

Serve the prawns immediately, garnished with the coriander sprigs and accompanied by the lime wedges, if wished.

chilli-marinated prawns with avocado sauce

ingredients

SERVES 4

650 g/1 lb 7 oz large raw
  prawns, shelled, deveined
  and tails left intact
1/2 tsp ground cumin
1/2 tsp mild chilli powder
1/2 tsp paprika
2 tbsp orange juice
grated rind of 1 orange
2 tbsp extra-virgin olive oil
2 tbsp chopped fresh
  coriander, plus extra
  to garnish
salt and pepper
2 ripe avocados
1/2 onion, finely chopped
1/4 fresh green or red chilli,
  deseeded and chopped
juice of 1/2 lime

method

Preheat the barbecue. Combine the prawns with the cumin, chilli powder, paprika, orange juice and rind, oil and half the coriander. Season to taste with salt and pepper.

Thread the prawns onto metal skewers, or bamboo skewers that have been soaked in cold water for 30 minutes.

Cut the avocados in half around the stone. Twist apart, then remove the stone with a knife. Carefully peel off the skin, then dice the flesh. Immediately combine the avocados with the remaining coriander, onion, chilli and lime juice in a non-metallic bowl. Season to taste with salt and pepper and set aside.

Place the prawns over the hot coals of the grill and cook for only a few minutes on each side, or until bright pink and opaque.

Serve the prawns garnished with chopped coriander and accompanied by the avocado sauce.

fish burritos

ingredients

SERVES 4–6

about 450 g/1 lb firm-fleshed
    white fish, such as red
    snapper or cod
salt and pepper
1/4 tsp ground cumin
pinch of dried oregano
4 garlic cloves, finely chopped
125 ml/4 fl oz fish stock or
    water mixed with 1 fish
    stock cube
juice of 1/2 lemon or lime
8 flour tortillas
2–3 romaine lettuce leaves,
    shredded
2 ripe tomatoes, diced
1 quantity salsa cruda (see
    page 168)
lemon slices, to serve

method

Season the fish to taste with salt and pepper, then place
in a saucepan with the cumin, oregano, garlic and
enough stock to cover.

Bring to the boil, then cook for 1 minute. Remove the
pan from the heat. Let the fish cool in the cooking liquid
for 30 minutes.

Remove the fish from the liquid with a slotted spoon and
break up into bite-size pieces. Place in a non-metallic
bowl, sprinkle with the lemon juice and set aside.

Heat the tortillas in an unoiled non-stick frying pan,
sprinkling them with a few drops of water as they heat;
wrap the tortillas in foil or a clean tea towel as you work
to keep them warm.

Arrange shredded lettuce in the centre of one tortilla,
spoon on a few big chunks of the fish, then sprinkle with
the tomatoes. Add some of the salsa cruda. Repeat with
the other tortillas and serve at once with lemon slices.

fish tacos ensenada-style

ingredients

SERVES 4

about 450 g/1 lb firm-fleshed
    white fish, such as red
    snapper or cod
1/4 tsp dried oregano
1/4 tsp ground cumin
1 tsp mild chilli powder
2 garlic cloves, finely chopped
salt and pepper
3 tbsp plain flour
vegetable oil, for frying
1/4 red cabbage, thinly sliced
    or shredded
juice of 2 limes
hot pepper sauce or salsa,
    to taste
8 corn tortillas (see page 206)
1 tbsp chopped fresh
    coriander
1/2 onion, chopped (optional)
salsa of your choice

method

Place the fish on a plate and sprinkle with half the oregano, cumin, chilli powder and garlic, and salt and pepper to taste. Dust with the flour.

Heat the oil in a frying pan until it is smoking, then fry the fish in several batches until it is golden on the outside and just tender in the middle. Remove from the pan and place on kitchen paper to drain.

In a non-metallic bowl, combine the cabbage with the remaining oregano, cumin, chilli powder and garlic, then stir in the lime juice and salt and hot pepper sauce to taste. Set aside.

Heat the tortillas in an unoiled non-stick frying pan, sprinkling with a few drops of water as they heat; wrap the tortillas in foil or a clean tea towel as you work to keep them warm. Alternatively, heat through in a stack in the pan, alternating the tortillas from the top to the bottom so that they warm evenly.

Place some of the warm fried fish in each tortilla with a large spoonful of the hot cabbage salad. Sprinkle with coriander and onion, if using. Add some salsa and serve immediately.

fish & refried bean tostadas with green salsa

ingredients

SERVES 4

about 450 g/1 lb firm-fleshed
    white fish, such as red
    snapper or cod
125 ml/4 fl oz fish stock
1/4 tsp ground cumin
1/4 tsp mild chilli powder
pinch of dried oregano
4 garlic cloves, finely chopped
salt and pepper
juice of 1/2 lemon or lime
8 soft corn tortillas
vegetable oil, for frying
400 g/14 oz canned refried
    beans, warmed with 2 tbsp
    water to thin
salsa of your choice
2–3 romaine lettuce leaves,
    shredded
3 tbsp chopped fresh
    coriander
2 tbsp chopped onion

to garnish

soured cream
chopped fresh herbs

method

Place the fish in a saucepan with the stock, cumin, chilli powder, oregano, garlic and salt and pepper to taste. Stir and gently bring to the boil, then immediately remove the pan from the heat. Let the fish cool in the cooking liquid.

When cool enough to handle, remove the fish from the liquid with a slotted spoon; reserve the cooking liquid. Break the fish up into bite-size pieces, place in a non-metallic bowl, sprinkle with the lemon juice and set aside until required.

To make the tostadas, fry the tortillas in a small amount of oil in a non-stick frying pan until crisp. Spread the tostadas evenly with the warmed refried beans.

Gently reheat the fish with a little of the reserved cooking liquid in a saucepan, then spoon the fish on top of the beans. Top each tostada with some of the salsa, lettuce, coriander and onion. Garnish each one with a generous spoonful of soured cream and a sprinkling of chopped fresh herbs. Serve the tostadas immediately.

chilli-prawn tacos

ingredients

SERVES 4

600 g/1 lb 5 oz raw prawns, shelled and deveined

2 tbsp chopped fresh flat-leaf parsley

12 tortilla shells

spring onions, chopped, to garnish

soured cream, to serve

taco sauce

1 tbsp olive oil

1 onion, finely chopped

1 green pepper, deseeded and diced

1–2 fresh hot green chillies, such as jalapeño, deseeded and finely chopped

3 garlic cloves, crushed

1 tsp ground cumin

1 tsp ground coriander

1 tsp brown sugar

450 g/1 lb ripe tomatoes, peeled and coarsely chopped

juice of $1/2$ lemon

salt and pepper

method

To make the sauce, heat the oil in a deep frying pan over medium heat. Add the onion and cook for 5 minutes, or until softened. Add the pepper and chillies and cook for 5 minutes. Add the garlic, cumin, coriander and sugar and cook the sauce for a further 2 minutes, stirring.

Add the tomatoes, lemon juice and salt and pepper to taste. Bring to the boil, then reduce the heat and simmer for 10 minutes.

Stir in the prawns and parsley, cover and cook gently for 5–8 minutes, or until the prawns are pink and tender.

Meanwhile, place the tortilla shells, open-side down, on a baking sheet. Warm in a preheated oven, 180°C/350°F/Gas Mark 4, for 2–3 minutes.

To serve, spoon the prawn mixture into the tortilla shells and top with a spoonful of soured cream.

crab & avocado soft tacos

ingredients

SERVES 4

8 soft corn tortillas

1 avocado

lime or lemon juice, for tossing

4–6 tbsp soured cream

250–280 g/9–10 oz cooked
crabmeat

1/2 lime

1/2 fresh green chilli, such as
jalapeño or serrano,
deseeded and chopped or
thinly sliced

1 ripe tomato, deseeded
and diced

1/2 small onion, finely chopped

2 tbsp chopped fresh
coriander

salsa of your choice, to serve
(optional)

method

Heat the tortillas in an unoiled non-stick frying pan, sprinkling them with a few drops of water as they heat; wrap in foil or a clean tea towel as you work to keep them warm.

Cut the avocado in half around the stone. Twist apart, then remove the stone with a knife. Carefully peel off the skin from the avocado, slice the flesh and toss in lime juice to prevent discoloration.

Spread one tortilla with soured cream. Top with crabmeat, a squeeze of lime and a sprinkling of chilli, tomato, onion, coriander and avocado, adding a generous spoonful of salsa, if desired. Fold in the sides to form a cornet, repeat with the remaining tortillas and serve at once.

salpicon of crab

ingredients

SERVES 4

$1/4$ red onion, chopped

$1/2$–1 fresh green chilli,
    deseeded and chopped

juice of $1/2$ lime

1 tbsp cider or other fruit
    vinegar, such as raspberry

1 tbsp chopped fresh
    coriander

1 tbsp extra-virgin olive oil

225–350 g/8–12 oz fresh
    crabmeat

lettuce leaves, to serve

to garnish

1 avocado

lime juice, for tossing

1–2 ripe tomatoes

3–5 radishes

method

In a large, non-metallic bowl, combine the red onion
with the chilli, lime juice, vinegar, coriander and oil. Add
the crabmeat and toss the ingredients lightly together.

To make the garnish, cut the avocado in half around the
stone. Twist apart, then remove the stone with a knife.
Carefully peel off the skin and slice the flesh. Toss the
avocado gently in lime juice to prevent discoloration.

Halve the tomatoes, then remove the cores and seeds.
Dice the flesh. Thinly slice the radishes.

Arrange the crab salad on a bed of lettuce leaves and
garnish with the avocado, tomatoes and radishes.
Serve at once.

citrus-marinated fish

ingredients

SERVES 4

450 g/1 lb white-fleshed fish fillets, cut into bite-size chunks

juice of 6–8 limes

2–3 ripe flavourful tomatoes, diced

3 fresh green chillies, such as jalapeño or serrano, deseeded and thinly sliced

$^1\!/_2$ tsp dried oregano

4 tbsp extra-virgin olive oil

1 small onion, finely chopped

salt and pepper

2 tbsp chopped fresh coriander

method

Place the fish in a non-metallic dish, add the lime juice and mix well. Cover and chill in the refrigerator for 5 hours, or until the fish looks opaque. (Do not leave too long, otherwise the texture will spoil.) Turn from time to time so that the lime juice permeates the fish.

An hour before serving, add the tomatoes, chillies, oregano, oil and onion. Season to taste with salt and pepper. Return to the refrigerator.

About 15 minutes before serving, remove from the refrigerator so that the oil comes to room temperature. Serve sprinkled with coriander.

ceviche salad

ingredients

SERVES 4

450 g/1 lb salmon, red snapper
   or sole fillets, skinned and
   cut into strips or slices
1 small onion, finely chopped
1 fresh jalapeño chilli or
   2 small fresh mild green
   chillies, deseeded and
   finely chopped
juice of 3 limes
1 tbsp extra-virgin olive oil
1 tbsp chopped fresh
   coriander, plus extra to
   garnish
1 tbsp snipped fresh chives
   or dill
salt and pepper
2 tomatoes, peeled and diced
shredded crisp lettuce.
2 tbsp capers, rinsed
   (optional)

method

Place the fish, onion, chilli, lime juice, oil and herbs in
a non-metallic dish and mix together. Cover and chill in
the refrigerator for 8 hours or overnight, stirring occasionally
to ensure that the fish is well coated in the marinade.

When ready to serve, remove the dish from the refrigerator
and season to taste with salt and pepper.

Arrange the fish mixture on top of shredded crisp lettuce
on a large serving plate. Sprinkle the capers over the
mixture and sprinkle with chopped coriander to garnish.

on the side

The Mexicans really know how to spice things up a bit, as you will discover in this chapter. There are recipes for the most amazing salsas, vegetables and salads, as well as for rice dishes with a difference, and for cooking beans – including Mexico's famous 'refried beans', which feature in many recipes.

Beans are a staple in Mexican cooking and in every marketplace café and home kitchen there will be a pot of simmering beans, ready to be added to a typical recipe or simply eaten from a bowl with a few tortillas. The types of beans used vary throughout the country, from the tender pale pink beans of the north, such as pinto, to the inky black beans of the south.

Salsas also appear on every table in every corner of Mexico – made of vegetables and fruits, raw, cooked, chopped, chunky, smooth, spicy, mild or fiery, they add interest, colour, texture and flavour. Sauces have a similar role – do be sure to try Mole Poblano, the classic sauce of chillies and chocolate!

At the end of this chapter you will find a recipe for flour tortillas, the thin, pancake-like flat breads. They are remarkably easy to make and will bring a special touch of authenticity to your Mexican menu.

black bean nachos

ingredients

SERVES 4

225 g/8 oz dried black beans,
    or canned black beans,
    drained
175–225 g/6–8 oz grated
    cheese, such as Cheddar,
    fontina, romano, Asiago
    or a combination
about 1/4 tsp cumin seeds or
    ground cumin
about 4 tbsp soured cream
thinly sliced pickled jalapeño
    chillies (optional)
1 tbsp chopped fresh
    coriander
handful of shredded lettuce
tortilla chips, to serve

method

If using dried black beans, soak the beans overnight,
then drain. Put into a saucepan, cover with water, and
bring to the boil. Boil for 10 minutes, then reduce the
heat and simmer for 1 1/2 hours, or until tender.
Drain well.

Spread the beans in a shallow ovenproof dish, then
scatter the cheese over the top. Sprinkle with cumin to
taste.

Bake in a preheated oven, 190°C/375°F/Gas Mark 5, for
10–15 minutes, or until the beans are cooked through
and the cheese is bubbly and melted.

Remove from the oven and spoon the soured cream on
top. Add the chillies, if using, and sprinkle with
coriander and lettuce.

Arrange the tortilla chips around the beans, placing
them in the mixture. Serve the nachos at once.

guacamole

ingredients

SERVES 4

2 large, ripe avocados

juice of 1 lime, or to taste

2 tsp olive oil

$1/2$ onion, finely chopped

1 fresh green chilli, such as
poblano, deseeded and
finely chopped

1 garlic clove, crushed

$1/4$ tsp ground cumin

1 tbsp chopped fresh
coriander, plus extra to
garnish (optional)

salt and pepper

method

Cut the avocados in half lengthways and twist the halves in opposite directions to separate. Stab the stone with the point of a sharp knife and lift out.

Peel, then coarsely chop the avocado halves and place in a non-metallic bowl. Squeeze over the lime juice and add the oil.

Mash the avocados with a fork until the desired consistency – either chunky or smooth. Blend in the onion, chilli, garlic, cumin and chopped coriander, then season to taste with salt and pepper.

Transfer to a serving dish and serve at once, to avoid discoloration, sprinkled with extra chopped coriander, if liked.

coriander mayonnaise

ingredients

SERVES 4

1 egg

2 tsp prepared mustard

1/2 tsp salt

squeeze of lemon juice

2 tbsp chopped fresh
    coriander

1 fresh mild green chilli,
    deseeded and finely
    chopped

300 ml/10 fl oz olive oil

method

Place the egg in a food processor or blender, add the
mustard and salt and process for 30 seconds.

Add the lemon juice, coriander and chilli and process
briefly.

With the motor still running, add the olive oil through the
feeder tube in a thin, steady stream. The mixture will
thicken after half the oil has been added.

Continue adding the remaining oil until it is all absorbed.
Transfer to a serving bowl, cover and chill in the
refrigerator for 30 minutes to allow the flavours to
develop before serving.

mole verde

ingredients

SERVES 4–6

250 g/9 oz toasted pumpkin
seeds

1 litre/32 fl oz chicken stock

several pinches of ground
cloves

8–10 tomatillos, diced, or use
225 ml/8 fl oz mild
tomatillo salsa

1/2 onion, chopped

1/2 fresh green chilli,
deseeded and diced

3 garlic cloves, chopped

1/2 tsp fresh thyme leaves

1/2 tsp fresh marjoram leaves

3 tbsp shortening or
vegetable oil

3 bay leaves

4 tbsp chopped fresh
coriander

salt and pepper

fresh green chilli slices,
to garnish

method

Grind the toasted pumpkin seeds in a food processor.
Add half the stock, the cloves, tomatillos, onion, chilli,
garlic, thyme and marjoram and blend to a purée.

Heat the shortening in a heavy-based frying pan and
add the puréed pumpkin seed mixture and the bay
leaves. Cook over medium–high heat for 5 minutes, or
until the mixture begins to thicken.

Remove the pan from the heat and add the remaining
stock and the coriander. Return the pan to the heat and
cook until the sauce thickens, then remove from the heat.

Remove the bay leaves, place the sauce in a food
processor or blender and process until completely
smooth. Add salt and pepper to taste.

Transfer to a serving bowl, garnish with chilli slices
and serve.

mole poblano

ingredients

SERVES 4

3 dried mulato chillies

3 mild dried ancho chillies

5–6 dried New Mexico or
   California chillies

1 onion, chopped

5 garlic cloves, chopped

450 g/1 lb ripe tomatoes

2 tortillas, preferably stale, cut
   into small pieces

pinch of cloves

pinch of fennel seeds

1/8 tsp each ground cinnamon,
   coriander and cumin

3 tbsp lightly toasted sesame
   seeds or tahini

3 tbsp slivered or coarsely
   ground blanched almonds

2 tbsp raisins

1 tbsp peanut butter (optional)

500 ml/16 fl oz chicken stock

3–4 tbsp grated plain
   chocolate, plus extra
   to garnish

2 tbsp mild chilli powder

3 tbsp vegetable oil

salt and pepper

about 1 tbsp lime juice

method

Using metal tongs, roast each chilli over an open flame
for a few seconds until the colour darkens on all sides.
Alternatively, roast in an unoiled frying pan over medium
heat for 30 seconds, turning constantly.

Place the roasted chillies in a heatproof bowl and pour
over enough boiling water to cover. Cover with a lid and let
soften for at least 1 hour or overnight. Once or twice, lift
the lid and rearrange the chillies so that they soak evenly.

Remove the softened chillies with a slotted spoon.
Discard the stalks and seeds and cut the flesh into
pieces. Place in a food processor or blender.

Add the onion, garlic, tomatoes, tortillas, cloves, fennel
seeds, cinnamon, coriander, cumin, sesame seeds,
almonds, raisins and peanut butter, if using, then
process to combine. With the motor running, add enough
stock through the feed tube to make a smooth paste.
Stir in the remaining stock, chocolate and chilli powder.

Heat the oil in a heavy-based saucepan until it is
smoking, then pour in the mole mixture. It will splatter
and pop as it hits the hot oil. Cook for 10 minutes, stirring
occasionally to prevent it burning.

Season to taste with salt, pepper and lime juice, garnish
with a little grated chocolate and serve.

mild red chilli sauce

ingredients

MAKES ABOUT 300 ML/ 10 FL OZ

5 large fresh mild chillies, such as New Mexico or ancho

500 ml/16 fl oz vegetable or chicken stock

1 tbsp masa harina or 1 crumbled corn tortilla, puréed with enough water to make a thin paste

large pinch of ground cumin

1–2 garlic cloves, finely chopped

juice of 1 lime

salt (optional)

method

Using metal tongs, roast each chilli over an open flame for a few seconds until the colour darkens on all sides. Alternatively, place the chillies under a preheated hot grill, turning them frequently. Place the chillies in a heatproof bowl and pour boiling water over them. Cover and let the chillies cool.

Meanwhile, place the stock in a saucepan and bring to a simmer.

When the chillies have cooled and are swelled up and softened, remove from the water. Remove the seeds, then cut the flesh into pieces. Process to a purée in a food processor or blender, then mix in the hot stock.

Place the chilli and stock mixture in a pan. Add the masa harina or puréed tortilla, cumin, garlic and lime juice. Bring to the boil and cook for a few minutes, stirring, until the sauce has thickened. Add salt to taste, if necessary, and serve.

quick tomato sauce

ingredients

SERVES 4–6

2 tbsp vegetable or olive oil

1 onion, thinly sliced

5 garlic cloves, thinly sliced

400 g/14 oz canned
    tomatoes, diced, plus their
    juices, or 600 g/1 lb 5 oz
    fresh diced tomatoes

several shakes of mild chilli
    powder

300 ml/10 fl oz vegetable
    stock

salt and pepper

method

Heat the oil in a large frying pan. Add the onion and
garlic and cook for 3 minutes, or until just softened,
stirring constantly.

Add the tomatoes, chilli powder to taste and the stock.
Cook over medium–high heat for 10 minutes, or until
the tomatoes have reduced slightly and the flavour of
the sauce is more concentrated.

Season the sauce to taste with salt and pepper. Serve
the dish warm.

chipotle salsa

ingredients

**MAKES ABOUT 500 ML/
16 FL OZ**

450 g/1 lb ripe juicy
    tomatoes, diced

3–5 garlic cloves, finely
    chopped

1/2 bunch fresh coriander
    leaves, coarsely chopped

1 small onion, chopped

1–2 tsp adobo marinade from
    canned chipotle chillies

1/2–1 tsp sugar

lime juice, to taste

salt

pinch of ground cinnamon
    (optional)

pinch of ground allspice
    (optional)

pinch of ground cumin
    (optional)

method

Place the tomatoes, garlic and coriander in a food
processor or blender.

Process the mixture until smooth, then add the onion,
adobo marinade and sugar.

Squeeze in lime juice to taste. Season to taste with salt,
then add the cinnamon, allspice and cumin, if using.

Serve at once, or cover and chill until ready to serve,
although the salsa is at its best when served freshly made.

corn and red pepper salsa

ingredients

SERVES 4–6

450 g/1 lb canned sweetcorn
 kernels

1 large red pepper, diced

1 garlic clove, crushed

1–2 tbsp finely chopped
 bottled jalapeño chillies,
 or to taste

4 spring onions, finely
 chopped

2 tbsp lemon juice

1 tbsp olive oil

1 tbsp chopped fresh
 coriander

salt

method

Drain the sweetcorn and place in a large, non-metallic bowl.

Add the red pepper, garlic, chillies, spring onions, lemon juice, oil and chopped coriander, then season to taste with salt and stir well to combine.

Cover and chill in the refrigerator for at least 30 minutes to allow the flavours to develop before serving.

two classic salsas

ingredients

SERVES 4–6

jalapeño salsa

1 onion, finely chopped

2–3 garlic cloves, finely chopped

4–6 tbsp coarsely chopped pickled jalapeño chillies

juice of 1/2 lemon

about 1/4 tsp ground cumin

salt

salsa cruda

6–8 ripe tomatoes, finely chopped

100 ml/31/2 fl oz tomato juice

3–4 garlic cloves, finely chopped

1/2–1 bunch fresh coriander leaves, coarsely chopped

pinch of sugar

3–4 fresh green chillies, such as jalapeño or serrano, deseeded and finely chopped

1/2–1 tsp ground cumin

3–4 spring onions, finely chopped

salt

method

To make the jalapeño salsa, place the onion in a non-metallic bowl with the garlic, chillies, lemon juice and cumin. Season to taste with salt and stir together. Cover and chill until required.

To make a chunky-textured salsa cruda, stir all the ingredients together in a non-metallic bowl, adding salt to taste. Cover and chill until required.

To make a smoother-textured salsa, process the ingredients in a food processor or blender. Cover and chill until required.

pico de gallo salsa

ingredients

SERVES 4–6

3 large, ripe tomatoes

$1/2$ red onion, finely chopped

1 large fresh green chilli,
    such as jalapeño,
    deseeded and
    finely chopped

2 tbsp chopped fresh
    coriander

juice of 1 lime, or to taste

salt and pepper

method

Halve the tomatoes, scoop out and discard the seeds and dice the flesh. Place the flesh in a large, non-metallic bowl.

Add the onion, chilli, chopped coriander and lime juice. Season to taste with salt and pepper and stir gently to combine.

Cover and chill in the refrigerator for at least 30 minutes to allow the flavours to develop before serving.

pineapple &
mango salsa

ingredients

SERVES 4

1/2 ripe pineapple

1 ripe mango

2 tbsp chopped fresh mint

2 tsp brown sugar

juice of 1 lime

1–2 tsp Tabasco sauce or
   Habañero sauce, or
   to taste

1 large tomato, deseeded
   and diced

salt

method

Slice the pineapple, then peel the slices and remove the cores. Dice the flesh and place in a non-metallic bowl with any juice.

Slice the mango lengthways on either side of the flat central stone. Peel the 2 mango pieces and dice the flesh. Slice and peel any remaining flesh around the stone, then dice. Add to the pineapple with any juice.

Add the chopped mint, sugar, lime juice, Tabasco and tomato, then season to taste with salt and stir well to combine. Cover and chill in the refrigerator for at least 30 minutes to allow the flavours to develop. Stir again before serving.

summer squash with green chillies & corn

ingredients

SERVES 4–6

2 corn cobs

2 small courgettes or other
   green summer squash,
   such as pattypans, cubed
   or sliced

2 small yellow summer
   squash, cubed or sliced

2 tbsp butter

3 garlic cloves, finely chopped

3–4 large ripe flavourful
   tomatoes, diced

several pinches of mild chilli
   powder

several pinches of ground
   cumin

1/2 fresh green chilli, such
   as jalapeño, deseeded and
   chopped

pinch of sugar

salt and pepper

method

Bring about 5 cm/2 inches of water to the boil in the
bottom of a steamer. Add the corn, courgettes and
summer squash to the top part of the steamer, cover and
steam for about 3 minutes, depending on their maturity
and freshness. Alternatively, blanch in a pan of boiling
salted water for 3 minutes, then drain. Set aside until cool
enough to handle.

Using a large knife, slice the kernels off the cobs and set
aside.

Melt the butter in a heavy-based frying pan. Add the
garlic and cook for 1 minute to soften. Add the tomatoes,
chilli powder, cumin, chilli and sugar. Season to taste
with salt and pepper and cook for a few minutes, or until
the flavours have mingled.

Add the corn kernels, courgettes and squash. Cook for
2 minutes, stirring, to warm through. Serve at once.

courgette & summer squash with chorizo

ingredients

SERVES 4

2 courgettes, thinly sliced

2 yellow summer squash, thinly sliced

2 fresh chorizo sausages, diced or sliced

3 garlic cloves, finely chopped

juice of $1/2$–1 lime

salt and pepper

1–2 tbsp chopped fresh coriander

method

Cook the courgettes and summer squash in a saucepan of boiling salted water for 3–4 minutes, or until they are just tender. Drain well.

Brown the chorizo in a heavy-based frying pan, stirring with a spoon to break up into pieces. Pour off any excess fat from the browned chorizo, then add the garlic and blanched courgettes and summer squash. Cook for a few minutes, stirring gently, to combine the flavours.

Stir in the lime juice to taste. Season with salt and pepper and serve at once sprinkled with chopped coriander.

courgette with green chilli vinaigrette

ingredients

SERVES 4

1 large fresh mild green chilli
or a combination of 1 green
pepper and $^1/_2$–1 fresh
green chilli

4 courgettes, sliced

2–3 garlic cloves, finely
chopped

pinch of sugar

$^1/_4$ tsp ground cumin

2 tbsp white wine vinegar

4 tbsp extra-virgin olive oil

2–3 tbsp chopped fresh
coriander

salt and pepper

4 ripe tomatoes, diced or sliced

tortilla chips, to serve (optional)

method

Roast the chilli, or the combination of the green pepper and chilli, in an unoiled heavy-based frying pan or under a preheated hot grill until the skin is charred. Place in a plastic bag, twist to seal well and set aside for 20 minutes.

Peel the skin from the chilli and pepper, if using, then remove the seeds and slice the flesh. Set aside.

Bring about 5 cm/2 inches of water to the boil in the bottom of a steamer. Add the courgettes to the top part of the steamer, cover and steam for 5 minutes, or until just tender.

Meanwhile, thoroughly combine the garlic, sugar, cumin, vinegar, oil and coriander in a bowl. Stir in the chilli and pepper, if using, then season to taste with salt and pepper.

Arrange the courgettes and tomatoes in a serving bowl or on a platter and spoon over the chilli dressing. Toss gently and serve with tortilla chips, if wished.

potatoes with chipotle cream

ingredients

SERVES 4

1.25 kg/2 lb 12 oz baking
   potatoes, peeled and cut
   into chunks
pinch of salt
pinch of sugar
200 ml/7 fl oz soured cream
125 ml/4 fl oz vegetable or
   chicken stock
3 garlic cloves, finely chopped
few shakes of bottled chipotle
   salsa or $^1/_2$ dried chipotle,
   reconstituted, deseeded
   and thinly sliced
225 g/8 oz goat's cheese,
   sliced
175 g/6 oz mozzarella or
   Cheddar cheese, grated
50 g/1$^3/_4$ oz Parmesan or
   romano cheese, grated

method

Place the potatoes in a saucepan of water with the salt and sugar. Bring to the boil and cook for 10 minutes, or until they are half cooked.

Combine the soured cream with the stock, garlic and the chipotle salsa in a bowl.

Arrange half the potatoes in a flameproof casserole. Pour half the soured cream sauce over the potatoes and cover with the goat's cheese slices. Top with the remaining potatoes and the sauce.

Sprinkle with the grated mozzarella or Cheddar cheese, then with either the grated Parmesan or romano cheese.

Bake in a preheated oven, 180°C/350°F/Gas Mark 4, for 30 minutes, or until the potatoes are tender and the cheese topping is lightly golden and crisp in places. Serve at once.

potatoes in green sauce

ingredients

SERVES 6

1 kg/2 lb 4 oz small waxy
potatoes, peeled

salt

1 onion, halved and unpeeled

8 garlic cloves, unpeeled

1 fresh green chilli

8 tomatillos, outer husks
removed, or small tart
tomatoes

225 ml/8 fl oz chicken, meat,
or vegetable stock,
preferably home-made

1/2 tsp ground cumin

1 fresh thyme sprig or
generous pinch of dried
thyme

1 fresh oregano sprig or
generous pinch of dried
oregano

2 tbsp vegetable or virgin
olive oil

1 courgette, coarsely chopped

1 bunch fresh coriander,
chopped

method

Place the potatoes in a saucepan of salted water. Bring
to the boil and cook for 15 minutes, or until almost
tender. Do not overcook them. Drain and set aside.

Lightly char the onion, garlic, chilli and tomatillos or
tomatoes in an unoiled heavy-based frying pan. Set
aside. When cool enough to handle, peel and chop the
onion, garlic and chilli; chop the tomatillos or tomatoes.
Place in a food processor or blender with half the stock
and process to form a purée. Add the cumin, thyme and
oregano and stir well to combine.

Heat the oil in the heavy-based frying pan. Add the
purée and cook for 5 minutes, stirring, to reduce slightly
and concentrate the flavours.

Add the potatoes and courgette to the purée and pour
in the rest of the stock. Add about half the coriander
and cook for a further 5 minutes, or until the courgette
is tender.

Transfer to a serving bowl and serve sprinkled with the
remaining chopped coriander to garnish.

citrus salad with pomegranate

ingredients

SERVES 4

1 large pomegranate

1 grapefruit

2 sweet oranges

finely grated rind of $^1/_2$ lime

1–2 garlic cloves, finely
    chopped

3 tbsp red wine vinegar

juice of 2 limes

$^1/_2$ tsp sugar

$^1/_4$ tsp dry mustard

salt and pepper

4–5 tbsp extra-virgin olive oil

1 head red leafy lettuce, such
    as oak leaf, washed and
    dried

1 avocado, pitted, peeled,
    diced, and tossed with a
    little lime juice

$^1/_2$ red onion, thinly sliced,
    to garnish

method

Cut the pomegranate into quarters, then press back the
outer skin to push out the seeds into a bowl.

Using a sharp knife, cut a slice off the top and bottom
of the grapefruit, then remove the peel and pith, cutting
downward. Cut out the segments from between the
membranes, then add to the pomegranate.

Finely grate the rind of half an orange and set aside.
Using a sharp knife, cut a slice off the top and bottom
of both oranges, then remove the peel and pith, cutting
downward and taking care to retain the shape of the
oranges. Slice horizontally into slices, then cut into
fourths. Add the oranges to the pomegranate and
grapefruit and stir to mix well.

Combine the reserved orange rind with the lime rind,
garlic, vinegar, lime juice, sugar and mustard in a small
non-metallic bowl. Season to taste with salt and pepper,
then whisk in the oil.

Place the lettuce leaves in a serving bowl, then top
with the fruit mixture and the avocado. Pour over the
dressing and toss gently. Garnish with the onion rings
and serve at once.

papaya, avocado & red pepper salad

ingredients

SERVES 4–6

200 g/7 oz mixed salad leaves

2–3 spring onions, chopped

3–4 tbsp chopped fresh
coriander

1 small papaya

2 red peppers

1 avocado

1 tbsp lime juice

3–4 tbsp pumpkin seeds,
preferably toasted
(optional)

dressing

juice of 1 lime

large pinch of paprika

large pinch of ground cumin

large pinch of sugar

1 garlic clove, finely chopped

4 tbsp extra-virgin olive oil

salt

dash of white wine vinegar
(optional)

method

Combine the salad leaves with the spring onions and coriander in a bowl. Mix well, then transfer the salad to a large serving dish.

Cut the papaya in half and scoop out the seeds with a spoon. Cut into quarters, remove the peel and slice the flesh. Arrange on top of the salad leaves. Cut the peppers in half, remove the cores and seeds, then thinly slice. Add the peppers to the salad leaves.

Cut the avocado in half around the stone. Twist apart, then remove the stone with a knife. Carefully peel off the skin, dice the flesh and toss in lime juice to prevent discoloration. Add to the other salad ingredients.

To make the dressing, whisk the lime juice, paprika, cumin, sugar, garlic and oil together in a small bowl. Season to taste with salt.

Pour the dressing over the salad and toss lightly, adding a dash of wine vinegar if a flavour with more 'bite' is preferred. Sprinkle with pumpkin seeds, if using.

mexican
potato salad

ingredients

SERVES 4

1.25 kg/2 lb 12 oz waxy
    potatoes, sliced

1 ripe avocado

1 tsp olive oil

1 tsp lemon juice

1 garlic clove, crushed

1 onion, chopped

2 large tomatoes, sliced

1 fresh green chilli, deseeded
    and chopped

1 yellow pepper, deseeded
    and sliced

2 tbsp chopped fresh
    coriander

salt and pepper

lemon wedges, to garnish

method

Cook the potato slices in a saucepan of boiling water for
10–15 minutes, or until tender. Drain and cool.

Meanwhile, cut the avocado in half, remove the stone
and peel. Mash the avocado flesh with a fork (you could
also scoop the avocado flesh from the 2 halves using a
spoon and then mash it).

Add the olive oil, lemon juice, garlic and chopped onion
to the avocado flesh and stir to mix. Cover the bowl with
clingfilm, to minimize discoloration, and set aside.

Combine the tomatoes, green chilli and yellow pepper and
transfer to a salad bowl with the potato slices.

Arrange the avocado mixture on top of the salad and
sprinkle with the chopped fresh coriander. Season to
taste with salt and pepper and serve the salad
immediately, garnished with lemon wedges.

green bean salad with feta cheese

ingredients

SERVES 4

350 g/12 oz green beans

1 red onion, chopped

3–4 tbsp chopped fresh
    coriander

2 radishes, thinly sliced

75 g/2³/4 oz feta cheese
    (drained weight), crumbled

1 tsp chopped fresh oregano,
    plus extra leaves to garnish
    (optional), or ¹/2 tsp dried

pepper

2 tbsp red wine or fruit vinegar

6 tbsp extra-virgin olive oil

3 ripe tomatoes, cut into
    wedges

method

Bring about 5 cm/2 inches of water to the boil in the
bottom of a steamer. Add the beans to the top part of
the steamer, cover and steam for 5 minutes, or until
just tender.

Place the beans in a large bowl and add the onion,
coriander, radishes and feta cheese.

Sprinkle the oregano over the salad, then season to taste
with pepper. Mix the vinegar and oil together in a small
bowl and pour over the salad. Toss gently to mix well.

Transfer to a serving platter, surround with the tomato
wedges and serve at once, or cover and chill until ready
to serve.

rice with lime

ingredients

SERVES 4

2 tbsp vegetable oil

1 small onion, finely chopped

3 garlic cloves, finely chopped

175 g/6 oz long-grain rice

500 ml/16 fl oz chicken or
   vegetable stock

juice of 1 lime

1 tbsp chopped fresh
   coriander

sautéed plantain, to garnish
   (optional)

lime wedges, to serve
   (optional)

method

Heat the oil in a flameproof casserole or heavy-based saucepan. Add the onion and garlic and cook gently, stirring occasionally, for 2 minutes. Add the rice and cook for a further minute, stirring. Pour in the stock, increase the heat and bring the rice to the boil. Reduce the heat to a very low simmer.

Cover and cook the rice for 10 minutes, or until the rice is just tender and the liquid is absorbed.

Sprinkle in the lime juice and fork the rice to fluff up and to mix in the juice. Sprinkle with the coriander, then garnish with sautéed plantain and serve with lime wedges, if wished.

spicy rice

ingredients

SERVES 4

3 tbsp olive oil

6 spring onions, chopped

1 celery stalk, finely chopped

3 garlic cloves, finely chopped

2 green peppers, deseeded
and chopped

corn kernels, cut from 1 ear
fresh corn

2 fresh mild green chillies,
deseeded and finely
chopped

250 g/9 oz long-grain rice

2 tsp ground cumin

600 ml/20 fl oz chicken or
vegetable stock

2 tbsp chopped fresh
coriander

salt and pepper

fresh coriander sprigs,
to garnish

method

Heat the oil in a large, heavy-based saucepan over
medium heat. Add the spring onions, celery and garlic
and cook for 5 minutes, or until softened. Add the
peppers, corn and chillies and cook for 5 minutes.

Add the rice and cumin and cook, stirring to coat the
grains in the oil, for 2 minutes.

Stir in the stock and half the chopped coriander and
bring to the boil. Reduce the heat, cover and simmer for
15 minutes, or until nearly all the liquid has been absorbed
and the rice is just tender.

Remove from the heat and fluff up with a fork. Stir in the
remaining chopped coriander and season to taste with
salt and pepper. Let stand, covered, for 5 minutes
before serving. Serve garnished with coriander sprigs.

rice with black beans

ingredients

SERVES 4

1 onion, chopped

5 garlic cloves, chopped

225 ml/8 fl oz chicken or
    vegetable stock

2 tbsp vegetable oil

175 g/6 oz long-grain rice

225 ml/8 fl oz liquid from
    cooking black beans,
    plus a few beans

$1/2$ tsp ground cumin

salt and pepper

to garnish

3–5 spring onions, thinly
    sliced

2 tbsp chopped fresh
    coriander

method

Place the onion in a food processor or blender with the garlic and stock and process until the consistency of a chunky sauce.

Heat the oil in a heavy-based frying pan and cook the rice until it is golden. Add the onion mixture with the cooking liquid from the black beans and any beans. Add the cumin and salt and pepper to taste.

Cover the pan and cook over medium–low heat for 10 minutes, or until the rice is just tender. The rice should be a pinkish-grey colour and taste delicious.

Fluff up the rice with a fork, then cover and let stand for 5 minutes. Serve sprinkled with thinly sliced spring onions and chopped coriander.

green rice

ingredients

SERVES 4

1–2 onions, unpeeled and
halved

6–8 large garlic cloves,
unpeeled

1 large mild fresh chilli or
1 green pepper and
1 small fresh green chilli

1 bunch fresh coriander
leaves, chopped

225 ml/8 fl oz chicken or
vegetable stock

6 tbsp vegetable or olive oil

175 g/6 oz long-grain rice

salt and pepper

fresh coriander sprig, to
garnish

method

Heat an unoiled heavy-based frying pan and cook the
onion, garlic, chilli and pepper, if using, until lightly charred
on all sides, including the cut sides of the onions. Cover
and cool.

When cool enough to handle, remove the skin and seeds
from the chilli and pepper, if using. Chop the flesh.

Remove the skins from the cooled onion and garlic and
finely chop.

Place the vegetables in a food processor or blender with
the chopped coriander leaves and stock, then process
to a smooth thin purée.

Heat the oil in a heavy-based saucepan. Add the rice
and cook until it is glistening and lightly browned in
places, stirring to prevent it burning. Add the vegetable
purée, cover and cook over medium–low heat for 10–15
minutes, or until the rice is just tender.

Fluff up the rice with a fork, then cover and let stand
for 5 minutes. Adjust the seasoning, garnish with a
coriander sprig and serve.

mexican beans

ingredients

SERVES 4

500 g/1 lb 2 oz dried pinto
    or pink beans
1 fresh mint sprig
1 fresh thyme sprig
1 fresh flat-leaf parsley sprig
1 onion, cut into chunks
salt
shredded spring onion, to
    garnish
warmed flour tortillas (see
    page 206) or soft corn
    tortillas, to serve

method

Pick through the beans and remove any bits of grit
or stone. Cover the beans with cold water and soak
overnight. If you want to cut down on soaking time, bring
the beans to the boil in a saucepan, cook for 5 minutes,
then remove from the heat and let stand, covered, for
2 hours.

Drain the beans, place in a saucepan and cover with
fresh water. Add the herb sprigs. Bring to the boil, then
reduce the heat to very low and cook gently, covered, for
2 hours, or until the beans are tender. The best way to
check that they are done is to sample a bean or two every
so often after $1^3/_4$ hours' cooking time.

Add the onion chunks and continue to cook until the
onion and beans are very tender.

To serve as a side dish, drain, season to taste with salt
and serve in a bowl lined with warmed tortillas, garnished
with shredded spring onion.

refried beans

ingredients

SERVES 4

225 g/8 oz dried pinto beans,
    soaked overnight and
    drained

2 onions, 1 quartered and
    1 chopped

1 chopped and 1 whole
    bay leaf

1 fresh thyme sprig

1 dried red chilli, such as
    ancho

3 tbsp olive oil

2 tsp ground cumin

85 g/3 oz Cheddar cheese,
    grated (optional)

method

Place the beans in a large saucepan with the quartered onion, herbs and chilli. Pour over enough cold water to cover and bring to the boil. Reduce the heat, cover and simmer gently for 2 hours, or until the beans are very tender.

Drain the beans, reserving the cooking liquid, and discard the onion, herbs and chilli.

Place two-thirds of the beans with the cooking liquid in a food processor or blender and process until coarsely blended.

Heat the oil in a heavy-based frying pan over medium heat. Add the chopped onion and cook for 10 minutes, or until soft and golden. Add the cumin and cook, stirring, for 2 minutes. Stir in the puréed and reserved beans and cook, stirring constantly, until the liquid reduces and the mixture thickens. Stir in the grated cheese, if using, and cook, stirring, until melted. Serve at once.

chilli cornbread

ingredients

SERVES 8

140 g/5 oz cornmeal

70 g/2 1/2 oz plain flour

3 tsp baking powder

1 small onion, finely chopped

1–2 fresh green chillies, such
as jalapeño, deseeded and
chopped

4 tbsp corn or vegetable oil

125 g/4 1/2 oz canned
creamed-style sweetcorn
kernels

225 ml/8 fl oz soured cream

2 eggs, beaten

method

Place the cornmeal, flour and baking powder in a large bowl, then stir in the onion and chilli.

Heat the oil in a 23-cm/9-inch heavy-based frying pan with a heatproof handle, tipping the pan to coat the bottom and sides with the oil.

Make a well in the centre of the ingredients in the bowl. Add the corn, soured cream and eggs, then pour in the hot oil from the frying pan. Stir lightly until combined. Pour into the hot pan and smooth the surface.

Bake in a preheated oven, 180°C/350°F/Gas Mark 4, for 35–40 minutes, or until a wooden cocktail stick inserted into the centre comes out clean. Cut into wedges and serve warm from the pan.

flour tortillas

ingredients

MAKES 12

350 g/12 oz plain flour, plus
    extra for dusting

1 tsp salt

$1/2$ tsp baking powder

75 g/$2^3/4$ oz shortening or
    white vegetable fat, diced

about 125 ml/4 fl oz hot water

method

Sift the flour, salt and baking powder into a large bowl.
Add the shortening and rub it in with your fingertips until
the mixture resembles fine breadcrumbs. Add enough
water to form a soft dough.

Turn out the dough onto a lightly floured work surface
and knead until smooth. Divide the dough into 12 pieces
and shape each into a ball. Cover with a clean tea towel
and let rest for 15 minutes.

Roll out 1 ball at a time, keeping the remainder of the
dough covered, into an 18-cm/7-inch circle. Stack the
tortillas between sheets of non-stick baking parchment.

Heat a griddle pan or large, heavy-based frying pan
over medium–high heat. Cook 1 tortilla at a time for 1–2
minutes on each side, or until lightly browned in places
and puffed up. Serve warm.

to finish

After the hearty and satisfying fare that is characteristic of Mexico, you might find that all you want to finish your meal is some fresh fruit, served Mexican-style with a splash of tequila or a squeeze of lime to flavour it. If you need something to counter the effects of the hot spices, serve the fruit frozen and whipped into a 'blizzard' or made into a refreshing sorbet. An incredible variety of fruits is grown in Mexico, from citrus fruits to melons and pineapples, mangoes and papaya, peaches and plums – just choose your favourite.

Those with a very sweet tooth will find plenty to satisfy their cravings – a delicious chocolate crème caramel, melt-in-the-mouth chocolate meringues, pastries bursting with fruity fillings, or puffy deep-fried bunuelos, a sort of doughnut, served in a puddle of orange-cinnamon syrup. There is also the light and wonderful *torta de cielo* – it is surely impossible to resist anything with a name that translates into 'cake of heaven' and tastes as good as it sounds.

There are some interesting blends of ingredients here and there – Mexican bread pudding is topped with cheese, for example, and if you're a fan of chocolate-chip ice cream, beware, because that unique chocolate/chilli combo creeps in here, too!

icy fruit blizzard

ingredients

SERVES 4

1 pineapple

1 large piece deseeded
    watermelon, peeled and
    cut into small pieces

225 g/8 oz strawberries or
    other berries, hulled and
    left whole or sliced

1 mango, peach or nectarine,
    peeled and sliced

1 banana, peeled and sliced

orange juice

caster sugar, to taste

method

Cover 2 baking sheets with a sheet of clingfilm. Arrange the fruits on top and open freeze for at least 2 hours, or until firm and icy.

Place one type of fruit in a food processor and process until it is all broken up into small pieces.

Add a little orange juice and sugar to taste, and continue to process until it forms a granular mixture. Repeat with the remaining fruits. Arrange in chilled bowls and serve immediately.

guava, lime & tequila sorbet

ingredients

SERVES 4

175 g/6 oz caster sugar

425 ml/15 fl oz water

4 fresh ripe guavas or 8 canned guava halves

2 tbsp tequila

juice of 1/2 lime, or to taste

1 egg white

method

Heat the sugar and water in a heavy-based saucepan over low heat until the sugar has dissolved. When the liquid turns clear, boil for 5 minutes, or until a thick syrup forms. Remove the pan from the heat and let cool.

Cut the fresh guavas, if using, in half. Scoop out the flesh. Discard the seeds from the fresh or canned guava flesh. Transfer to a food processor or blender and process until smooth.

Add the purée to the syrup with the tequila and lime juice to taste. Transfer the mixture to a freezerproof container and freeze for 1 hour, or until slushy.

Remove from the freezer and process again until smooth. Return to the freezer and freeze until firm. Process again until smooth. With the motor still running, add the egg white through the feeder tube. Freeze until solid.

Transfer the sorbet to the refrigerator 15 minutes before serving. Serve in scoops.

chocolate chip
& chilli ice cream

ingredients

SERVES 4

1 egg

1 egg yolk

55 g/2 oz caster sugar

150 g/5^1/$_2$ oz plain chocolate,
    finely chopped

550 ml/18 fl oz milk

1 dried red chilli, such as
    ancho

1 vanilla bean

550 ml/18 fl oz double cream

150 g/5^1/$_2$ oz plain, milk or
    white chocolate chips

method

Place the egg, egg yolk and sugar in a heatproof bowl
set over a saucepan of simmering water. Beat until light
and fluffy.

Place the chopped chocolate, milk, chilli and vanilla
bean in a separate saucepan and heat gently until
the chocolate has dissolved and the milk is almost
boiling. Pour onto the egg mixture, discarding the chilli
and vanilla bean, and beat well. Let cool.

Lightly whip the cream in a separate bowl. Fold into the
cold mixture with the chocolate chips. Transfer to an ice
cream machine and process for 15 minutes, or according
to the manufacturer's instructions. Alternatively, transfer
to a freezerproof container and freeze for 1 hour, or until
partially frozen. Remove from the freezer, transfer to a
bowl and beat to break down the ice crystals. Freeze
again for 30 minutes, then beat again. Freeze once
more until firm.

Transfer the ice cream to the refrigerator 15 minutes
before serving. Serve in scoops.

mexican chocolate crème caramel

ingredients

SERVES 4

115 g/4 oz granulated sugar

4 tbsp water

600 ml/20 fl oz milk

2 oz/55 g plain chocolate, grated

4 eggs

2 tbsp caster sugar

1 tsp vanilla essence

method

Preheat the oven to 160°C/325°F/Gas Mark 2½. Place a 1-litre/32-fl oz soufflé dish in the oven to heat.

Place the granulated sugar and water in a heavy-based saucepan over low heat. Stir until the sugar has dissolved. Bring to the boil, without stirring, and boil until caramelized. Pour into the hot dish, tipping it to coat the bottom and sides. Let cool.

Place the milk and grated chocolate in a separate saucepan and heat, stirring occasionally, until the chocolate has dissolved.

Meanwhile, beat the eggs and caster sugar together in a bowl with a wooden spoon. Gradually beat in the chocolate milk. Add the vanilla essence. Strain into the prepared dish.

Stand the dish in a roasting pan and fill the pan with enough lukewarm water to come halfway up the sides of the dish. Bake in the preheated oven for 1 hour, or until set. Let cool, then invert onto a serving plate. Chill in the refrigerator before serving.

oranges &
strawberries
with lime

ingredients

SERVES 4

3 sweet oranges
225 g/8 oz strawberries
grated rind and juice of 1 lime
1–2 tbsp caster sugar
fine lime rind strips and a
    fresh mint sprig,
    to decorate

method

Using a sharp knife, cut a slice off the top and bottom of the oranges, then remove the peel and pith, cutting downward and taking care to retain the shape of the oranges.

Using a small sharp knife, cut down between the membranes of the oranges to remove the segments. Discard the membranes.

Hull the strawberries, pulling the leaves off with a pinching action. Cut into slices, along the length of the strawberries.

Place the oranges and strawberries in a non-metallic bowl, then sprinkle with the lime rind and juice and sugar. Cover and chill until ready to serve.

To serve, transfer to a serving bowl. Decorate the dish with lime rind strips and a mint sprig.

aztec oranges

ingredients

SERVES 4–6

6 oranges

1 lime

2 tbsp tequila

2 tbsp orange-flavoured
    liqueur

brown sugar, to taste

fine lime rind strips,
    to decorate

method

Using a sharp knife, cut a slice off the top and bottom of the oranges, then remove the peel and pith, cutting downward and taking care to retain the shape of the oranges.

Holding the oranges on their side, cut them horizontally into slices.

Place the oranges in a non-metallic bowl. Cut the lime in half and squeeze over the oranges. Sprinkle with the tequila and liqueur, then sprinkle over sugar to taste.

Cover and chill until ready to serve, then transfer to a serving dish and garnish with lime rind strips.

pineapple with tequila & mint

ingredients

SERVES 4–6

1 ripe pineapple

sugar, to taste

juice of 1 lemon

2–3 tbsp tequila or a few
    drops of vanilla essence

several sprigs of fresh mint,
    leaves removed and cut
    into thin strips

fresh mint sprig, to decorate

method

Using a sharp knife, cut off the top and bottom of the pineapple. Place upright on a board, then slice off the skin, cutting downward. Cut in half, remove the core if wished, then cut the flesh into chunks.

Place the pineapple in a bowl and sprinkle with the sugar, lemon juice and tequila or vanilla essence.

Toss the pineapple to coat well, then cover and chill until ready to serve.

To serve, arrange on a serving plate and sprinkle with the mint strips. Decorate the dish with a mint sprig.

bunuelos with orange-cinnamon syrup

ingredients

SERVES 4

225 g/8 oz plain flour, plus extra for dusting

1 tsp baking powder

1/4 tsp salt

1 tbsp brown sugar

1 egg, beaten

2 tbsp butter, melted

125 ml/4 fl oz evaporated milk

vegetable oil, for deep-frying

orange-cinnamon syrup

350 ml/12 fl oz water

grated rind of 1 small orange

4 tbsp freshly squeezed orange juice

100 g/3 1/2 oz brown sugar

1 tbsp honey

2 tsp ground cinnamon

method

Sift the flour, baking powder and salt together into a large bowl. Stir in the sugar. Beat in the egg and butter with enough evaporated milk to form a soft, smooth dough. Shape the dough into 8 balls. Cover and let rest for 30 minutes.

Meanwhile, to make the syrup, place the water, orange rind and juice, sugar, honey and cinnamon in a heavy-based saucepan over medium heat. Bring to the boil, stirring constantly, then reduce the heat and simmer gently for 20 minutes, or until thickened.

Flatten the dough balls to make cakes. Heat the oil for deep-frying in a deep-fryer or deep saucepan to 180–190°C/350–375°F, or until a cube of bread browns in 30 seconds. Deep-fry the bunuelos in batches for 4–5 minutes, turning once, or until golden brown and puffed. Remove with a slotted spoon and drain on kitchen paper. Serve with the syrup spooned over.

empanadas of banana & chocolate

ingredients

SERVES 4 – 6

about 8 sheets of filo pastry,
    cut in half lengthways

melted butter or vegetable oil,
    for brushing

2 ripe sweet bananas

1–2 tsp sugar

juice of 1/4 lemon

175–200 g/6–7 oz plain
    chocolate, broken into
    small pieces

icing sugar, for dusting

ground cinnamon, for dusting

method

Working one at a time, lay a long rectangular sheet of filo out in front of you and brush it with butter.

Peel and dice the bananas and place in a bowl. Add the sugar and lemon juice and stir well to combine. Stir in the chocolate.

Place a couple of teaspoons of the banana and chocolate mixture in one corner of the dough, then fold over into a triangle shape to enclose the filling. Continue to fold in a triangular shape, until the filo is completely wrapped around the filling.

Dust the pockets with icing sugar and cinnamon. Place on a baking sheet and continue the process with the remaining filo and filling.

Bake in a preheated oven, 190°C/375°F/Gas Mark 5, for 15 minutes, or until the pastries are golden. Remove from the oven and serve hot – warn people that the filling is very hot.

peach & pecan empanadas

ingredients

MAKES 8

350 g/12 oz ready-made puff
   pastry, thawed if frozen
plain flour, for dusting
3 fresh peaches
150 ml/5 fl oz soured cream
4 tbsp brown sugar
4 tbsp pecan halves, toasted
   and finely chopped
beaten egg, to glaze
caster sugar, for sprinkling

method

Roll out the pastry on a lightly floured work surface.
Using a 15-cm/6-inch saucer as a guide, cut out
8 circles.

Place the peaches in a heatproof bowl and pour over
enough boiling water to cover. Let stand for a few
seconds, then drain and peel off the skins. Halve the
peaches, remove the stones and slice the flesh.

Place a spoonful of soured cream on one half of each
pastry circle and top with a few peach slices. Sprinkle
over a little brown sugar and some nuts. Brush each
edge with a little beaten egg, fold the pastry over the
filling and press the edges together to seal. Crimp the
edges with a fork and prick the tops.

Place on a baking sheet, brush with beaten egg and
sprinkle with caster sugar. Bake in a preheated oven,
200°C/400°F/Gas Mark 6, for 20 minutes, or until they
turn golden brown.

churros

ingredients

SERVES 4

225 ml/8 fl oz water

85 g/3 oz butter or
    shortening, diced

2 tbsp brown sugar

finely grated rind of 1 small
    orange (optional)

pinch of salt

175 g/6 oz plain flour, well
    sifted

1 tsp ground cinnamon, plus
    extra for dusting

1 tsp vanilla essence

2 eggs

vegetable oil, for deep-frying

caster sugar, for dusting

method

Heat the water, butter, brown sugar, orange rind, if
using, and salt in a heavy-based saucepan over medium
heat until the butter has melted.

Add the flour, all at once, the cinnamon and vanilla
essence, then remove the pan from the heat and beat
rapidly until the mixture pulls away from the side of
the pan.

Let cool slightly, then beat in the eggs, one at a time,
beating well after each addition, until the mixture is thick
and smooth. Spoon into a pastry bag fitted with a wide
star tip.

Heat the oil for deep-frying in a deep-fryer or deep
saucepan to 180°–190°C/350°–375°F, or until a cube of
bread browns in 30 seconds. Pipe 13-cm/5-inch lengths
about 7.5 cm/3 inches apart into the oil. Deep-fry for
2 minutes on each side, or until golden brown. Remove
with a slotted spoon and drain on kitchen paper.

Dust the churros with caster sugar and cinnamon and
serve immediately.

mexican bread pudding

ingredients

SERVES 4

350 ml/12 fl oz water
225 g/8 oz brown sugar
1 cinnamon stick, broken
1 tsp ground anise
55 g/2 oz raisins
55 g/2 oz butter, plus extra
    for greasing
10 small slices bread
85 g/3 oz shelled pecans,
    toasted and chopped
55 g/2 oz slivered almonds,
    toasted
175 g/6 oz mild Cheddar
    cheese, grated

method

Heat the water, sugar, cinnamon stick and anise in a saucepan over medium heat and stir constantly until the sugar has dissolved. Add the raisins and simmer for 5 minutes without stirring.

Spread butter onto one side of each bread slice and arrange buttered-side up on a baking sheet. Bake in a preheated oven, 190°C/375°F/Gas Mark 5, for 5 minutes, or until golden brown. Turn over and bake the other side for 5 minutes.

Line the base of a generously greased ovenproof dish with half the toast. Sprinkle over half the nuts and grated cheese. Remove and discard the cinnamon stick from the raisin mixture, then spoon half of the raisin mixture over the toast. Top with the remaining toast, nuts, grated cheese and raisin mixture.

Bake in the oven for 20–25 minutes, or until set and golden brown on top.

mexican chocolate meringues

ingredients

MAKES ABOUT 25 MERINGUES

4–5 egg whites, at room
    temperature
pinch of salt
$1/4$ tsp cream of tartar
$1/4$–$1/2$ tsp vanilla essence
175–200 g/6–7 oz caster
    sugar
$1/8$–$1/4$ tsp ground cinnamon
115 g/4 oz plain chocolate,
    grated

to serve
ground cinnamon
115 g/4 oz strawberries
chocolate-flavoured cream

method

Whisk the egg whites until they are foamy, then add the salt and cream of tartar and beat until very stiff. Whisk in the vanilla essence, then slowly whisk in the sugar, a small amount at a time, until the meringue is shiny and stiff. This should take about 3 minutes by hand, and under a minute with an electric beater.

Whisk in the cinnamon and grated chocolate. Spoon mounds of about 2 tablespoonfuls on to an ungreased non-stick baking sheet. Space the mounds well.

Bake in a preheated oven, 150°C/300°F/Gas Mark 2, for 2 hours, or until set.

Carefully remove from the baking sheet. If the meringues are too moist and soft, return them to the oven to firm up and dry out more. Let cool completely.

Serve the chocolate meringues dusted with ground cinnamon and accompanied by strawberries and chocolate-flavoured cream.

mexican wedding cakes

ingredients

MAKES ABOUT 36

225 g/8 oz butter, softened
225 g/8 oz icing sugar
1 tsp vanilla essence
225 g/8 oz plain flour, plus
    extra for dusting
$1/2$ tsp salt
100 g/$3^1/2$ oz pecan or walnut
    halves, toasted and finely
    chopped

method

Cream the butter with half the sugar and vanilla essence in a large bowl. Sift the flour and salt together into the bowl and fold into the mixture. Stir in the nuts. Cover and chill in the refrigerator for 1 hour, or until firm.

With floured hands, shape the dough into 2.5-cm/1-inch balls and place about 4 cm/$1^1/2$ inches apart on 2 large baking sheets.

Bake in a preheated oven, 190°C/375°F/Gas Mark 5, for 10 minutes, or until set but not browned, rotating the baking sheets so that the biscuits bake evenly. Let cool on the baking sheets for 2–3 minutes.

Place the remaining sugar in a shallow dish. Roll the warm biscuits in the sugar, then cool on wire racks for 30 minutes. When cold, roll again in the sugar. Store in airtight containers.

torta de cielo

ingredients

SERVES 4–6

225 g/8 oz unsalted butter, at
room temperature, plus
extra for greasing
175 g/6 oz whole almonds, in
their skins
225 g/8 oz sugar
3 eggs, lightly beaten
1 tsp almond essence
1 tsp vanilla essence
9 tbsp plain flour
pinch of salt

to decorate

icing sugar, for dusting
slivered almonds, toasted

method

Lightly grease a 20-cm/8-inch round or square cake pan
and line the pan with baking parchment.

Place the almonds in a food processor and process to
form a 'mealy' mixture. Set aside.

Beat the butter and sugar together in a large bowl until
smooth and fluffy. Beat in the eggs, almonds and both
the almond and vanilla essences until well blended.

Stir in the flour and salt and mix briefly, until the flour is
just incorporated.

Pour or spoon the batter into the prepared pan and
smooth the surface. Bake in a preheated oven,
180°C/350°F/Gas Mark 4, for 40–50 minutes, or until
the cake feels spongy when gently pressed.

Remove from the oven and let stand on a wire rack
to cool. To serve, dust with icing sugar and decorate
with toasted slivered almonds.